THE DEVIL DECEPTION

BUT GOD'S GLORY

A HEAVEN AND HELL
REAL LIFE EXPERIENCE

Dr. Darryl K. Horne

STUDIO
OF BOOKS
THE SPACE FOR YOUR MESSAGE

Studio of Books LLC
5900 Balcones Drive Suite 100
Austin, Texas 78731
www.studioofbooks.org
Hotline: (254) 800-1183

Ordering Information:
Special discounts are available on quantity purchases by corporations, associations, and others. For details, contact the publisher at the address above.

Printed in the United States of America.

ISBN-13: Softcover 978-1-964864-36-5
            eBook 978-1-964864-37-2

Library of Congress Control Number: 2024916629

Dedication

This testimony is dedicated to the memory of my beloved parents, Ulysses and Barbara Horne, and my Lord and Savior, Jesus Christ. This book is a result of the foundational spiritual and academic goals that my mom set for me. I am grateful to her for her role in teaching me the values of life, the importance of an education, and most important teachings about Christ at a very early age. As a single parent of 11 children, she worked very hard to make sure we had everything we needed. She worked very diligently to see me through college, which provided me the educational tools I possess today. Thank you for being my hero. All I am today and all I will become in the future I owe to you. You have always provided me with inspiration, motivation, and the determination to strive for the best. This book is also dedicated to my family and friends, and all those who supported me through my life while helping guide me to spiritual joy.

Acknowledgments

A life's journey is not an easy journey. I am very fortunate and blessed to be sharing this testimony with you. First and foremost, I want to give thanks to my Lord and Savior, Jesus Christ for giving me the strength and knowledge to trial this journey. As I navigate through many challenges in my life, I give thanks to the many family members, friends, my pastor, bishop, and editor who supported me, and helped guide me along the path to completion. I want to give special thanks to Rena Marion for her research, support, motivation, inspiration, and editing assistance. I want to thank my wife, our children and grandchildren for helping make me the person, man, father, and poppa that I am today.

I want to give a personal thank you to my ten brothers and sisters. Thank you Brenda, the leader of the pack. She was the first born of the family and the first to go to "Glory" shortly after birth. Even though none of the siblings ever met her I frequently recognize and feel her presence. Thank you, Rick, for showing me what it means to be a father. Thank you, Deborah, for showing me how to fight the good fight and never quit. I consider you to be our family oracle. Thank you, Lin, for showing me how, and when to stand strong while fighting for what you believe. Thank you, Les, for showing me how to open my heart and home to anyone in need. Thank you, Mike for showing men the mechanics of life, and how to protect myself when being attacked. Thank you, Reece, for showing me strength, and being another living example for me of how, through faith, you can overcome anything. Thank you, Tanya "granny", for being the mother figure I needed once mom had gone to "Glory". Thank you, Stevie, for showing me what it means to endure. You have proven to everyone that united you stand and divided you fall. Thank you, Brian, for "showing me better than you can tell me"; you truly did and have. All of you have paved the way for me to travel, which being the youngest made my life easier, and helped guide my life's decisions. Without all of you only God knows where my life would be right now. I thank you all for being the best family ever, the best that anyone could ever want or need.

A personal note to my readers

I grew up on the eastside of Detroit just two blocks west of GrossPointe, near Jefferson Avenue. Up until the present, I have personally witnessed how a neighborhood or city can physically transform from life (vibrant, safe, beautiful and proud) to death (ruined, vandalized, abandoned, unsafe, worried, and broken). Even though I was "saved" as a young boy, I didn't "know" Jesus Christ. I never formally introduced myself to Him nor took the time to get to know Him until my adulthood, when "He" told me that I didn't know Him? As I began to fellowship with Him the more, He revealed to me, and our relationship began to evolve. The more it evolved, and the more I got involved, the more I got to know Him. He already knew me. As a matter of fact, as time went on He began to tell me things about myself that I did not know and even things that had not yet happened. Jesus wants to have a personal relationship with you, and the only way to do that is to talk to Him.

As my spiritual walk increased, the more I could see my spiritual transformation from death to life. Life in the spirit is so much better than life in the flesh. In the spirit you can do supernatural things, but in the flesh you can only do what is confined to the body. Matthew 6:33 says "seek ye first the kingdom of God, and His righteousness; and all these things shall be added unto you". The "things" being spoken of in this passage are the "things" of Christ. The only way to understand what those "things" are is to get to know Him. Seek first Him and all of His glory, honor and praise will be added unto you. Without Jesus Christ being the head of your life, and your source provider you are already physically and spiritually dead, you just don't know it or you just don't want to believe that He is who says He is. John 14:6 puts it very plain as Jesus Himself speaks by saying, "I am the way the truth and the life. No one comes to the Father except through me". You cannot get to know God the Father unless you are first introduced to His Son Jesus. Jesus loves you and I do too. That is why I am taking the time out to write you a personal note because this is personal to me, and it is extremely important to Jesus! I don't like what the devil (sin) has done to my family; I don't like what the devil (sin) has done to my city, the city of Detroit. I don't like what the devil (sin) has done to God's creation and you shouldn't like it either. As Christians, our job is to make "earth" as "it is in heaven". This God given assignment is also shared with us in the Bible as the prayer of Jesus to His Father in Matthew 6:9-13. It reads, "…Our Father which art in heaven, Hallowed be thy name. Thy kingdom come". Thy will be done in earth as it is in heaven. Give us this day our daily bread. And forgive us our debts, as we forgive our debtors. And lead us not into temptation, but deliver us from evil: For thine is the kingdom, and the power, and the glory, forever. Amen."

In 1 John 2:15 scripture states, "Love not the world, neither the things that are in the world, the love of the Father is not in him". If you know God, it is impossible not to love Him. If you don't know God, it is impossible to love. If you want to change your situation, your life, and make a mark in this world, start by accepting the mark of Christ our Lord and Savior and then help share His mark with this world! I hope this testimony makes a difference in your life. May God continue to bless you and keep you. He is patiently waiting for your introduction!

Contents

Here are some personal testimonies from others of how God has touched and changed their life.

"Taste and see that the Lord is good…" (Psalm 34:8, NIV)

"Trust in the Lord with all your heart and lean not on your own understanding: in all your ways acknowledge him, and he will make your paths straight…"
(Proverbs 3:5-6, NIV)

I, Deborah L. Horne, give God the Glory for healing me of cancer. I am a witness of God's grace and mercy. I believe therefore I speak.

In the summer of 2013, I had my first colonoscopy at the age of 64. Thank God for the doctors and the medical staff at Henry Ford Hospital, who removed the one large polyp from my colon. Three weeks later I received a phone call from the doctor, who told me the pathology report states that cancer was contained in the polyp. Several letters followed the phone contact with a confirmation and recommendation to follow up with colon rectal surgery to schedule a consultation with the surgeon.

At that time they thought the best plan of treatment would be to remove the right side of the colon. This was to reduce the chance of cancer spreading throughout the rest of my body. My faith with all the many prayers through the power of God touched me and the heart of the specialist and moved him to call for a meeting of the minds to review the films and images one more time. That was my saving grace! When I returned two weeks later, all were in agreement that the cancerous polyp had been removed. The second colonoscopy confirmed I do not have cancer. I am healed. I am a witness… " All things are possible with God." Mark 10:27

My faith with all the many prayers through the power of God touched me and the heart of the specialist and moved him to call for a meeting of the minds to review the films and images one more time. That was my saving grace!

When I returned two weeks later, all were in agreement that the cancerous polyp had been removed. The second colonoscopy confirmed I do not have cancer. I am healed. I am a witness…

" All things are possible with God." Mark 10:27

Introduction

It was loud and steady at first. Each beat began to get slower and slower. I could feel the life leaving me. Slowly; then came the final beat. My eyes opened to darkness. I could not tell where I was or what kind of room I was in, but the walls were close. The ceiling inches above my head and face. I could barely move my arms. I realized I was lying down on my back. I could breathe, but the oxygen was getting low. My lungs began to want for air. I was starting to suffocate. I needed to get out, to get some air. I needed to claw my way out of this place. I started scratching, clawing, pushing… nothing. I was trapped. Then I saw them. They ripped the lid off the wooden coffin that I was in and immediately began beating me to death. They looked human, in shape only. Their eyes were black marbles, surrounded by pools of red blood. I could feel their rage while being snatched from the box, and could feel the heavy blows to my head and body.

Repeatedly, I was thrown around like a rag doll. The kicks and the punches I tried to use in defending myself were not enough. They were trying to break my bones in the midst of stabbing me. Over and over, I suffered this abuse yet without any bones broken or loss of consciousness, the pain and torture I received was unimaginable. Just when I thought some relief would come from blacking out, I was choked awake. Together they said, "Every time you pass out, we are going to wake you up, and keep doing this to you, because you will never die!" At that moment, I realized I was in Hell.

CHAPTER 1

THE GOOD LIFE

I was living the dream. I was married to a woman I loved. I had three beautiful children. I had a house with a pool, which I believed to be a sign of status, two new cars, a job with a major corporation, and money in the bank. I was young, educated and still striving for more. A few years earlier, I had graduated from Michigan State University with my bachelors in Packaging Engineering. I was the first one in my immediate family to do so.

There were 10 of us raised by my mother. I was the youngest. My mom was so proud, and that's what I lived for, to make her proud of me. She had done so much for me and my siblings and that is why I wanted to do my best for her. And not just for her, but my brothers and sisters as well. I wanted to succeed for all of them. I wanted to show them that we didn't have to be poor. If they ever needed anything, they could come to me, and I could help them. I was making a pretty good salary. It was enough to take care of my family, but I wanted more, to do more, to be more, and to have more. So, I went back to school to get a master's degree in management (MSM) and a master's degree in business administration (MBA). I started working for a company in the area of financial planning. I had a thirst for knowledge. The more I knew, the more I could do. It was all a part of my plan: to be financially independent and retire at an early age, and at the same time help other people realize their financial dreams. But by my calculations, that wasn't going to be enough. I wanted to own property, so I bought some rental properties. This way, I could provide a home for those who were less fortunate or needed a place to live, and make a profit at the same time. Now, it was all working together for my good and the good of my family. I needed to be a success, and my idea of success was a nice house, a good job making six figures plus, supporting my family, nice new cars, and all the grown-up toys I wanted: boat, snow mobile, and the ability to travel the world. To obtain this success, I had to work hard. Nobody was going to give it to me. I learned that from my mother. I watched her go to work every day, catching the bus or catching a ride. She never had a driver's license. She worked long hours as a waitress, linen launderer, concessions worker, and supervisor at Cobo Hall in downtown Detroit. Then when she came home, she had to take care of the family. Prior to obtaining her job at Cobo Hall my mother use to iron clothes for a living to ensure we were all fed and our needs were being met to the best of her ability. It broke my heart to see her so run down every day and yet she still had a smile for us. I had promised myself that when I was grown, she would never have to work another day in her life. So I put in the long hours on the job and in school.

You see, I needed more degrees because they meant more opportunities, and I had to get all I could, take advantage of every opportunity, go through every door available that was going to lead me to my goal…. becoming a cash millionaire by the time I was 40 years old. How was I going to do that? First, I needed to make enough money to replace my income. I would accomplish that by not just working in the financial service industry, but also by owning real estate. You see, if I owned 20 houses and profited at least $250 per month that would bring in $5000 every month. This would allow me to quit my job, and free me up to do other things to make more money. It would also provide for a pretty good retirement. I was on my way. I was working the plan. My marriage was great, and I was successful. I was working towards my dream. I had it all planned out. How could I lose? Then the bottom began to fall out from under me.

I was always so busy, working outside of my home. I was spending less and less time with my wife, and daughter, and more time helping others, and chasing my dream. Appointments with potential new clients; calls all times of the day to work on the rental properties; family members who needed my help, homework, not to mention my 9 to 5 job, my wife, and daughter. I had taken on the world, and I was holding it in the palm of my hand. I had everything under control, and all my hard work was paying off. Everybody was happy and benefiting from my working "the plan", or so I thought. I was married at the age of 26. My idea of marriage: it was eternal, everlasting. My role: to be the head, which meant being the main financial provider, being a positive example for my family, to be there for them, to work for them, to live for them, to give them everything; and they had everything, but my time. What I hadn't realized is that I had allowed myself to be pulled in so many different directions. Not only had I taken on the role of supporting my relatives, but I was also supporting my wife's immediate family as well. I was the provider, the go-to guy, the one with the means to help everyone. If it was broken, I'd fix it. If you didn't have it, I'd get it for you or figure out a way. If you couldn't do it for yourself by yourself, I'd do it for you. Their problems became my problems, their issues, my issues. I felt obligated, whatever the problem or need to fix it, help it, make it right, be the hero or their "Savior". It started to take a toll on my marriage, on my body, on my mind.

I had begun to feel that I was spending so much time and money taking care of others, and I was starting to neglect my own. Others were reaping all the benefits of me taking care of everything, and I didn't think I was getting anything in return. I started to feel used, taken advantage of by all of these people I was helping. I was being stretched to the end, trying to please everybody, doing for everybody. Like a rubber band, I was being pulled little by little. Growing in size, being stretched too far, and it eventually snapped. That's what happened to me. I had reached my breaking point, and things changed. I stopped "doing" for the family because it was physically draining, and financially depleting. Because of this I was said to have "changed". I was viewed as "mean" and made to feel of little value. My wife and I being of different cultures did not help either.

Our cultural differences began to manifest in how we dealt with each other, how we viewed family and the role our relatives played in our lives. I felt if I weren't meeting the needs of her family, then they no longer had any use for me. I know that was not the case, but none the less that is how I felt. I had never felt 100% engrafted into that side of the family. Maybe that's why I was doing so much, trying so hard to fit in and be accepted. But it wasn't working the way I had planned. I could never do enough, be enough, nor give enough to be totally included. I was hurt, angry, and disappointed that I had failed; failed to be a real part of them, and not just a resource.

The years went by. I kept telling myself everything was fine. I was doing the right thing, working hard, making money. I had what I wanted, and I did it on my own. Nobody helped me, I did it. It was all by my hand. I had begun to sing my own praises. Yet over time, things began to change. Slowly at first, so I really couldn't see it. The "falling down" was gradual, and I thought I was handling all things as well as I always had done. At home with my wife, I was allowed to do whatever I wanted to the point where I felt like she didn't care. With me being gone so much, she must have felt like I didn't care. The marriage began to break down. No time spent together, no communication, and it felt like no love. On top of that, financially, I had begun to lose everything, because I had completely forgotten about GOD and discerned that He is the source. I lost sight of His purpose for me. I was losing all of my rental properties. It led to the loss of my primary home. One of my family members was suing me. I lost my job in financial services, and now my wife of 15 years no longer wanted to be married. I knew I had lost her forever. I was facing total devastation. Everything I had worked for was falling apart all around me, and I felt helpless. What I thought couldn't happen was happening. For the first time, I couldn't fix it. I couldn't make it right.

My mom became very sick with cancer. She was the only person I felt still believed in me. I couldn't lose her, but the cancer took her on March 3, 1998. She wasn't around to help me, to talk over things, to make sense of my life. I prayed to God and asked Him to help me understand what was going on in my life, to take the pain and depression that I was feeling away and put my life back together. The Lord did not say anything to me for a few years, but the devil constantly reminded me of how much of a failure I was, how I was worthless, and how I was losing everything. This included the most important thing to me in life, my wife.

The devil constantly reminded me that there was nothing that I could do about it. In less than six months, I would not have anything left. I would be divorced and everything we owned would be gone. I prayed to the Lord and He eventually answered me by stating in a very stern voice "You Don't Know Me Boy!" I said Lord, what do you mean I don't know you, of course I know you? He again stated, "You Don't Know Me Boy!" 1 Corinthians 1:21 reflects on knowing God:

"For after that in the wisdom of God the world by wisdom knew not God, it pleased God by the foolishness of preaching to save them that believe."

I said Lord, "what do you mean I don't know you Lord, I have gone to church all my life and have tried to be good and do good all my life." The Lord responded, "I have provided for you your entire life, I have educated you more than most, you have read thousands of books, but you have never read mine!" "You have been distracted, and have not been listening to me!" He told me that the only way I could get to know Him is to spend time with Him. For the very first time in my life I listened while God was talking to me. My ears were wide open. I was tentatively hearing, and listening to what He wanted to tell me. I asked Him again to help me understand what I am doing wrong and to please make it right.

The Lord did not respond, and I later realized why. At that time, I was not able, nor ready to receive what He was going to tell me, and the devil still was not finished with me. The devil again began to remind me of all my failures, the death of my dad, and now mom, and the slow final death of my marriage, the woman I loved more than anything. The devil constantly reminded me that my wife no longer wanted me, and tried to convince me that God wouldn't even talk to me. I felt I had no one to turn to for help. This time I needed a hero, someone to come and save me. I was at the lowest point in my life and I didn't want to live. If you do not have a relationship with Christ or lose sight of God, His mercy and love or stop calling on Him for all your needs, the devil will always come in and wreak havoc on your life. The devil had me right where he wanted and was about to deliver me one heavy blow.

CHAPTER 2

MY DEMONIC ATTACK

Depression had completely consumed my mind, body, and soul. I was not eating or sleeping, and I was thoroughly exhausted. I was having what doctors refer to as a nervous break down, and I did not even realize it. A very close friend of mine was going to take a trip to Cancun, and he asked me to come along. I told him I did not have any money. He told me not to worry about the money and he would take care of it. He was aware of some of the things that were going on in my life, and felt a trip would be good for me. We arrive in Cancun one week later, still depressed, but having the time of my life. I decided to bring some of the ashes from my mothers' cremation to Cancun with me to be scattered on the ocean shore. My mom loved to travel, but never had the opportunity to travel too much, now she was part of Cancun. I was in total bliss This is when the Lord decided I was ready to hear what He had to say to me. While I was mourning and walking on the beach He fully explained to me why my marriage had fallen apart. He explained and helped me fully understand the cultural differences that my wife at the time and I were experiencing. Most of what He said, I have to admit, I did not want to hear, but God knew I needed to hear it. I was very grateful that He took the time to educate me and answer my prayers. The devil also decided to take a trip to Cancun and finish off what he had started back at home. The devil immediately began attacking my mind, causing me confusion, headaches, and hallucinations. I thought someone had slipped something into my drink. Being a nondrinker, the tequila shots I was drinking were taking a toll on me. I became very fearful, paranoid and confused. The friends that were with me noticed I was acting strange. They tried as much as they could to help me, but at the time, none of us fully understood what was taking place. Fortunately for me we were coming home the next day.

That night I did not sleep at all. I was too afraid to sleep. The devil taunted and tormented me mentally all night. All I wanted to do was get home, where I felt safe, then I could talk to someone about what I was experiencing. It seemed like it took forever for us to board the plane home. Time could not have moved any slower. Once we boarded the plane I thought things would get better, but they only got worse. I began having panic attacks and started thinking that everyone on the plane was going to die. I was scared to death, and for the next four hours I had to endure this torture to the best of my ability until I got home. It was the worst and scariest plane ride I have ever had.

After we got off the plane, I raced to the baggage claim area, picked up my luggage and hurriedly awaited for the arrival of the airport parking lot bus to arrive and take us to the car. I called my wife to let her know that I was home. She was not excited about my return and almost gave me the impression that she hoped I never came back. I tried to tell her what I had been experiencing for the past day and a half, but she didn't care to listen.

I arrived at my friends' house where my car was parked, jumped in and raced home. I don't know how I was able to drive home. I was still confused, paranoid, depressed, exhausted, and by this time probably dehydrated as well. I tried calling my wife on the way home while in the car; all she wanted to do was argue. This was very strange to me, because in the 15 years that we were married and the 20 plus years that we had known one another, despite our differences and the challenges of life which we encountered, we never once argued.

When I arrived home, I could tell she was still mad and had not forgotten or gotten over the problems or concerns that she had before I left for my Cancun trip. I was still paranoid, acting strange or what most would consider abnormal. This abnormal behavior scared her as well as our three children. They did not understand why I was acting this way.

I heard a car drive up in my driveway and a knock at the door. This too was strange and startling to me because it was about 12:00 midnight. I was not expecting anyone and at this time of the night who could it possibly be…it was my sister. My wife had called her and informed her that I was acting strange. She was scared, she advised my sister to please come by and see about me. I tried explaining to my sister to the best of my mental ability what I was experiencing, and how I was feeling. I now understand that to her, I was talking very irrational and not making sense at all. This only exacerbated the problem which caused me further frustration. I again heard another knock at the door and to my realization; my wife had also called my niece.

I again, began to attempt to explain to my niece what I had just experienced while in Cancun and what I was experiencing at the time. She too was confused, didn't understand and could not relate to what I was going through. What they were trying to do was understand an irrational person, rationally. I now know you can't. All you can do is listen to them, try to keep them calm and reassure them that everything will be alright. The last thing you want to tell them is that they are "trippin", not making sense or babbling. To them, while in that state of mind they are making perfect sense and to them, everyone else is confused.

Mistake number one; I immediately told everyone in the house to leave, to get out of my house, wife and kids included. This was a mistake because no one was there to look after me. In my state of mind at the time, the last thing I needed was to be left alone. From about 12:50 am to 4:00 am the devil taunted me, constantly reminding me that I was worthless, not loved, useless, and better off dead. I was totally exhausted and physically at my weakest point in life. The devil never attacks you when you are physically or spiritually strong. He waits until you are physically and spiritually weak and then launches his attack.

I eventually yielded to the devil's deception. I allowed him to make me feel so humiliated that suicide was the only way out. Initially I did not want to die; I just wanted the pounding in my head and the pain in my head and heart to stop. I retrieved my 9mm glock from my dresser drawer and tried to chamber a round, but my Lord said, "Nope, not like that." The gun jammed. I then swallowed four pain pills to try to stop the excessive painful throbbing in my head. It was not working fast enough, so I decided to take the whole bottle. To make sure it worked, I followed it up with a second bottle of pills; in all I swallowed 60 plus pills. The devil wanted to make sure I was really done so he also convinced me to take a knife and stab myself in the chest not once, but twice. This was in an attempt to pierce my heart…and again, my Lord said, "Nope, not like that." My death would not be by a stabbing.

The pills I had ingested slowly began to take full effect, causing me to die slowly. Before I died, I remember staggering throughout the house, leaving trails of blood from my stab wounds everywhere. I was incoherent, delirious, exhausted, dizzy, and unable to stand. As I fell to the floor I realized I had gone too far. Death had a hold of me and there was no escaping. I tried calling on God, but mentally I was gone. Due to the toxins in my body, I would not have been able to follow God's instructions even if He had told me what to do. So, what did I do, I did the only thing that I could do. While in my bedroom, I crawled to my bookcase, because I could no longer walk, I reached up and grabbed a bible I had received when I graduated from the 8th grade; still fresh in the original box, hardly ever used or opened. I opened the bible, but the words were blurred. I was unable to read or call on God, I could barely think. The room was spinning. I drew the Bible close to my chest. Now in a fetal position, I patiently waited while life slowly left my body. I began to recite Psalm 100,

"Make a joyful noise unto the LORD, all ye lands. Serve the LORD with gladness: come before his presence with singing. Know yet hat the LORD heis GOD: it is he that hath made us, and not we ourselves; we are his people, and the sheep of his pasture. Enter into his gates with thanksgiving, and into his courts with praise: be thankful unto HIM, and bless his name. For the LORD is good; his mercy is everlasting; and his truth endureth to all generations."

I had memorized this verse when I was a kid and only God knew I would need it at this time of life, that's why He had me learn it some 27 years earlier. Now I realize what miracles are all about. While I was reciting the Psalm I could hear my heart beating slower and slower. As death patiently drew near I remember listening to my heart beat. I listened to every beat until it literally stopped beating.

The devil had temporarily succeeded. He had successfully caused a living "Hell" in my life. He had caused my physical death and was trying to deliver the final blow, "Spiritual" death. He wanted my soul, and God allowed him to lure me to hell where I would have to make the greatest choice of my life.

CHAPTER 3

MY HELL EXPERIENCE

I arrived in hell in total darkness. I was in a place that was very confined. I was lying on my back and had very little room to move around. I felt very claustrophobic. As I attempted to move my arms and hands, I could feel something in front of me, just inches from my face. It felt like a wall or some kind of barrier. Slowly, I began to lose my breath. I was starting to suffocate. The oxygen inside this strange place was gradually dissipating; I was having great difficulty breathing. I began to panic. I very desperately started fighting my way out. I started pushing upward with my hands and arms as hard as I could. My efforts were useless. I was suffocating and needed to get air. I started clawing and scratching my way out until my nails and fingers were bleeding. My fingers became painfully numb. I was about to die from a lack of oxygen and there was nothing I could do about it. Just before I was about to black out, I found the "coffin" lid that I was in being ripped open. As I began to regain my spiritual consciousness I realized I had been inside a wooden coffin. The coffin lid was ripped off by two demons who painfully yanked me out of the coffin. The demons were in human form. They had the strength of a thousand men. Their eyes were like black marbles surrounded by pools of red blood. I could feel their rage while being snatched from the box as I immediately began absorbing heavy blows to my head and body. Their intent was to hurt me, torture me, and kill me beyond my wildest imagination. At this point in time, I still did not understand what was going on or realize that I was in hell. I tried to the best of my ability to fight them back, to fight them off. I tried, punching and kicking them but my combative defense had no effect on these demonic creatures. While trying to fight back and being beaten to death they told me, "That stuff doesn't work down here." They were referring to my martial arts skills. At that time, I had studied martial arts for more than 24 years. I was trying to use every fighting technique that I had learned while in the natural, but none of that seemed to work in this strange place that I was in.

The two demons then took out very long butcher knives, twelve to eighteen inches in length and began stabbing me. I felt the pain from every thrust of their knives as the tips penetrated my chest and exited my back. I endured multiple stabs, cuts and excruciating pain throughout my entire body. As I was thrown around like a rag doll, being tortured to death and in a state of shock, I began to ponder, why am I not dying... why am I not dead? That is when I realized I was in hell.

I was under eternal pain and torture. There was nothing I could do. The demons tormented me so fiercely I passed out because the pain was so unbearable. I soon regained my consciousness by being strangled awake, only to be subjected to endless torture again. The demons told me, "every time you pass out or "die", we are going to wake you up, and keep doing this to you, because you will never die!"

These demons were sent to greet me in hell by the devil. They are considered to be his angels. Upon my arrival they were anxious and excited to greet me, eager to begin their torture. They hated me. They hated me because, even though I was in hell, they could see the Christ in me and like their "lord" the "devil" hated Christ, they too hated me. In hell, evil is all around you. They enjoyed torturing me and delighted in the pain I felt.

I then found myself in what I considered to be a lava pit. In this lava pit I found many humans, other saints that had gone astray or those who never accepted Christ while in the natural. Our bodies bobbed up and down, in the lava. I could hear hollering, moaning, and ear-piercing screams. There was a stench of burnt human flesh in the air. The temperature was unbearably hot, hotter than anything you could ever imagine. I convulsed and watched in amaze as our flesh was burnt from our bodies, exposing our blood and bones and expeditiously repeated it. This torturing process was continuously repeated. In hell you never die, death is eternal, and everlasting. In hell sinners continue to feel unimaginable and unbelievable pains forever. The pain and torment never, ever stops. You die forever, and literally experience death over and over again, not only one type of death, multiple types; a continuous death process. Everyone in the pit including myself was saying, "oh GOD."

Scripture says every knee will bow.

Isaiah 45: 23 states: "I have sworn by myself, the word is gone out of my mouth in righteousness, and shall not return, That unto me every knee shall bow, every tongue shall swear."

Romans 14:11 states, "For it is written, As I live, saith the Lord, every knee shall bow to me, and every tongue shall confess to GOD."

This revealed to me that as it is written in the Word, every knee will bow to GOD one way or another. Either you will bow to praise Him now or you will bow when you are in hell for not receiving Him and asking Him for mercy and forgiveness.

I then found myself all alone in the pit of hell, still bobbing up and down in this pool of what appeared to be lava. My skin was still burning from my body, now my blood and bones included. Every time I burned, my flesh reappeared only to repeat the process, over and over again. I tried blacking out, but that would have given me minimal comfort and relief.

There is no comfort or pain relief in hell. I tried to think good thoughts; there are no good thoughts in hell. I continued to call on GOD, not a call of prayer, but a call of mercy. This is when I had to make the greatest decision of my life. I closed my eyes to try to get a millisecond of relief and I saw the devil standing on the shore of the lava pit. He was red in color, pointy ears, and had a long tail with an arrow shaped tip on the end. He was revealed to me in the shape of the devil cartoon character that we saw on television during my youth. The devil was very muscular in stature.

The devil, with his arms folded began to mock and laugh at me. He asked me, "where is your GOD now?" The pain and torture had heightened to an unimaginable, and unbearable level. The pain was so unbelievable that I infinitely convulsed. I could no longer speak, but the devil could read my thoughts, and I could read his. He wanted me to denounce Christ and accept him. He told me telepathically, if I accepted him and rejected Christ the pain would stop. I knew this was a lie or false truth based on teachings I received while in the natural (alive on earth). I knew the devil was lying. There was no way he was going to get me to denounce Christ, even while in hell.

Scripture states in John 8:44

"Ye are of your father the devil, and the lusts of your father ye will do. He was a murderer from the beginning, and abode not in the truth, because there is no truth in Him. When he speaketh a lie, he speaketh of his own: for he is a liar, and the father of it."

I also knew from what I was taught that the devil only wanted to hurt me. John 10:10 states,

"The thief cometh not, but for to steal, and to kill, and to destroy: I am come that they might have life, and that they might have it more abundantly."

Thank God, that prior to this experience I did get to know Him and accepted Him as my Lord and Savior. I still would not submit to the devil and the pain, torment, and torture were mind bogglingly unbearable. I could not talk. All I could do is continue to fiercely convulse. As I shook, I told the devil "I would never reject Christ, and I did not care how long he tortured me I would never denounce my God!" Remember, this was all done telepathically. I did not verbally speak to Him. I was in too much pain.

The pain is so horrifying in hell that it is impossible to talk or think logically. Your main focus is solely on the pain you are experiencing and an overwhelming burning desire to have it stop.

I once again (telepathically), asked God for His mercy, to please take me from this place. My now spiritual body could not take anymore. I was getting weak and felt like I was going to collapse. Now please remember, there is no relief in hell. You feel weak, but there is no relief. In hell weakness is considered to be comforting. Hell is never, ever comforting. Please reference the following scriptures:

Matthew 8:12, "But the children of the kingdom shall be cast out into outer darkness: there shall be weeping and gnashing of teeth.

Matthew 13:42, "And shall cast them into a furnace of fire: there shall be wailing and gnashing of teeth."

Matthew 22:13, "Then said the king to the servants, Bind Him hand and foot, and take Him away, and cast Him into outer darkness, there shall be weeping and gnashing of teeth."

Luke 13:28, "There shall be weeping and gnashing of teeth, when ye shall see Abraham, and Isaac, and Jacob, and all the prophets, in the kingdom of God, and you yourselves thrust out."

Just when I was about to give up, I saw a bright tunnel of light, radiantly beaming down upon me. The light was so bright I could barely look upon it. Matthew 10:32-33 states,

"32 Whoever acknowledges me before others, I will also acknowledge before my Father in heaven. 33 But whoever disowns me before others, I will disown before my Father in heaven."

God stretched out His hand and raised me from the pits of hell. I was as a limp noodle, lifeless, but now at peace. I was so tired I could not move. The torture, torment and pain were gone. As I lay in Christ's hand, I felt myself being raised upwards. As I drew upward the light got brighter and brighter, and I got stronger and stronger. I continued to slowly move, ascending upward.

As I broke "Heavens Barrier" I could hear cheering, as if a celebration was taking place. The Angels were rejoicing because another soul had come home. Amen!

Luke 15:10, states, "In the same way, I tell you, there is rejoicing in the presence of the angels of God over one sinner who repents."

See readers, I had to make the greatest choice in my life. Now in the "spirit" I had to make a choice, to choose the devil or choose God. Even as a sinner in the natural, I did give my life to the Lord; I did acknowledge Him as my Lord and Savior. What would have happened if I never knew of God, chose not to receive His Holy Spirit or accept Him as my Lord and Savior? I will tell you what would have happened;

I would have died on March 3, 2002, not shared this testimony and be eternally burning in hell. God showed me mercy. He will show you mercy too if you ask. God is good, His mercy is everlasting, and His Truth endures through all generations.

1 Chronicles 16:34 says: "Give thanks to the LORD, for he is good; his love endures forever."

1 Chronicles 16:41 states: "With them were Heman and Jeduthun and the rest of those chosen and designated by name to give thanks to the LORD, for his love endures forever."

2 Chronicles 5:13 states: "The trumpeters and musicians joined in unison to give praise and thanks to the LORD. Accompanied by trumpets, cymbals and other instruments, the singers raised their voices in praise to the LORD and sang: He is good; his love endures forever."

Please give your life to Christ today so you won't go to hell and share with Him eternal life. When I arrived in Heaven I was greeted by an angel, and I was totally astonished at who that angel was.

CHAPTER 4

MY HEAVENLY SURPRISE

Heaven is full of God's Glory. When I arrived in heaven I was met by the most beautiful angel, my mother! My mom was there to greet me. I could not physically see her but I could see, feel, smell, and touch her in the spirit. I also felt my father, grandparents, uncles and aunts' presence. Everyone who had already gone to Glory was there. I did not see them, but I could feel them, feel their presence. I could not physically see God, but I could feel His presence all around me, completely encapsulated by His glory and love. In the "spirit" all of the saved look alike. We all blended together like one body, the body of Christ. The spiritual beings that I witnessed, me included, consisted of extremely bright bodies of light; so bright that it is almost blinding. When combined with all of the saints, the Father and Christ we look like one massive ball or surrounding light. We are all like the Father and Son. Imagine for a moment, if you could stick your head inside a light bulb; what you see is how we all looked, and when combined there is nothing but total brightness all around you. You can not distinguish one from another; we all come together as one. Genesis 41:38 states,

"So Pharaoh asked them, "Can we find anyone like this man, one in whom is the spirit of God?"

1 Samuel 18, "After David had finished talking with Saul, Jonathan became one in spirit with David, and he loved Him as Himself."

Proverbs 20:27 states, "The human spirit is the lamp of the LORD that sheds light on one's inmost being."

Isaiah 34:16, "Look in the scroll of the LORD and read: None of these will be missing, not one will lack her mate. For it is his mouth that has given the order, and his Spirit will gather them together."

Isaiah 42:1, "Here is my servant, whom I uphold, my chosen one in whom I delight; I will put my Spirit on Him, and he will bring justice to the nations."

2 Corinthians 4:5-6, "For what we preach is not ourselves, but Jesus Christ as Lord, and ourselves as your servants for Jesus' sake. 6 For God, who said, "Let light shine out of darkness," made his light shine in our hearts to give us the light of the knowledge of God's glory displayed in the face of Christ."

We are all spiritual beings in a human body. Our true nature is spirit not flesh.

I held my mothers' hand and gazed all around her to see what I had hoped for all my life. I was like a kid in a candy store. I could not believe I was talking to my mother, nor could I believe I was in heaven. I was over joyously happy and excited. I asked my mom, "So this is it?" I was referring to Heaven. Telepathically I was thinking, where is Isaac, Jacob, Moses and Abraham? I wanted to see everyone. There is a peace about Heaven that is impossible to describe. No pain, no torture, no tears, no heart ache or hurt; just joy, mercy, tranquility, glory…God!

Unlike hell, I immediately recognized where I was. Even before I saw my mom, my spirit recognized that I was home, in Heaven. My heart was pounding very fast. In my excitement my mom, still holding my hand said, "Son, you got to go back!" I, now confused and perplexed said, "go back, what do you mean, go back; I don't want to go back." I did not want to go back to the natural, earth, home where I lived in Michigan. She again in a very calm, but stern voice said, "Son, you got to go back."

Shaking my head vigorously, while screaming, "No, I don't want to go back." I found myself slowly being drawn away from my mother, out of heaven, back down that tunnel of bright light that brought me to heaven. Moments later I woke up in my bed, butt naked. My faithful dog, Storm was sitting at the foot of the bed with an expression on her face that said, "man, you were "trippin" last night, if only I could talk." I thought I had just experienced a horrible nightmare and an amazingly wonderful dream.

Everything that I have shared with you up to this point all occurred within a six-hour window on the night that I arrived home from my Cancun trip and kicked my family out of the house. Remember before I died, I had made several suicide attempts before succeeding by taking the 60 plus pills. Guess what, the pills were still in my system! Prior to taking the pills and dying, I remember being fully clothed. I don't recall ever taking them off.

As I climbed out of the bed, I noticed a large pool of regurgitation on the carpet near the foot of my bed, close to where I had fallen before I had taken my last breath just hours before. How did my clothes get removed? How did I get back in the bed? These are questions that I still ponder over and the Holy Spirit has not yet revealed the answers.

I slowly walked to the bathroom. I was feeling kind of groggy. I turned on the light and gazed into the mirror. I rubbed my eyes as to get clarity in my vision and noticed two puncture wounds in my chest. There was blood draining out of them and was running down my chest. I looked at my dog again and thought, "The dog must have scratched me?" I took some gauze and surgical tape out of the medicine cabinet and covered up my wound. At this point I could not remember what I had just experienced. All I knew was, what ever I had just experienced before I got out of bed was good, really good!

CHAPTER 5

THE devil`s TENACITY

While I was getting dressed for the day, reality was slowly beginning to take form. I was starting to regain my memory. I remembered, less than 6 hours prior my wife and I had a big fight, and I told her and the kids to get out of the house. I started remembering what had got me upset prior to throwing everyone out of the house the night before. The rage and anger I had the night before slowly began to return, and the devil had some unfinished business to resolve with me.

I went into my living room, ripped the phone out of the wall outlet and threw it so hard into an adjacent wall that it literally stuck in the wall. I then picked up one of our dining room chairs and threw it through the dining room double pane picture window. I walked to the garage, got in my car and sped off. The paranoia I was experiencing the night before was back. That strange feeling had come back upon me. The demons had returned.

I sporadically drove around my neighborhood at excessive speeds. I was starting to feel anger, rage, anxiety, paranoia, delusional as well as hallucinogenic. I became very afraid and defensive. This fear pushed me into what medical doctors call "flight" mode. "Flight" mode is the body's automatic, primitive, or inborn response that prepares the body to "flee" or "fight" from perceived harm, attack, or threat of survival.

1 Peter 5:8 states: "Be alert and of sober mind. Your enemy the devil prowls around like a roaring lion looking for someone to devour."

Leviticus 25:17 states: "Do not take advantage of each other, but fear your God. I am the LORD your God."

Deuteronomy 6:24, "The LORD commanded us to obey all these decrees and to fear the LORD our God, so that we might always prosper and be kept alive, as is the case today."

Matthew 10:27-31, "27 What I tell you in the dark, speak in the daylight; what is whispered in your ear, proclaim from the roofs. 28 Do not be afraid of those who kill the body but cannot kill the soul. Rather, be afraid of the One who can destroy both soul and body in hell. 29 Are not two sparrows sold for a penny? Yet not one of them will fall to the ground outside your Father's care. 30 And even the very hairs of your head are all numbered. 31 So don't be afraid; you are worth more than many sparrows."

FEAR GOD, NOT THE DEVIL

At this time, I was unaware I was being followed by a local police officer for the past several miles. Still in flight panic mode I pressed my accelerator to the floor, driving to speeds in excess of 100 miles an hour. This was through residential areas and busy business sections of the city. I was endangering myself and others. I remember coming to a complete stop at a traffic light. I began to panic, so I drove over the center lane into on-coming traffic in an attempt to make it to the expressway just a few hundred feet in front of me. Needless to say, I didn't make it. I drove head on into an oncoming truck. My chest hit the steering wheel and my head smashed against the windshield. Now, with toxins still in my system, scared, confused and pumped up on adrenaline, I jumped out of my car and leaped over the hood and I ran across the freeway overpass. I then proceeded to jump over the rail and dropped nearly 10 feet to the grass area parallel to the freeway. Remember, the police officer behind me is witnessing all of this. I can just imagine what he was thinking at that time. I stood on the grass stunned, stooped over, out of breathe, with my hands on my knees. My back was facing the overpass that I had just jumped from. I still hadn't realized the police were following me; now several squad cars. I remember being grabbed from behind and being put in a submissive choke hold. I could not see who was behind me. I then heard someone say, "Hit him!" Something hit my eyes and I was blinded. My eyes were starting to burn. I could not see anything in front, behind or around me. I wondered, "What in the heck just happened?" I heard the comment, "Hit him again!" This strange "stuff" again went into my eyes and the choke hold around my neck got even tighter.

I thought, "this must be the driver or the passengers in the truck I just hit?" I was beginning to choke again, just like I did when I was in the coffin in hell. I started fighting for my life. I started swinging, punching and kicking anything that I could feel. After what seemed to be an hour fight but was no more than a three minute struggle, I found myself being tackled by multiple individuals, and my face being pushed in the snow. My arms were wrenched around my back while hearing the sound of hand cuffs being tightened around my wrist. At that point I realized, it was not the individuals in the truck who were fighting with me, but several police officers.

Knowing they were police officers helped me relax. The front of the bright yellow fleece pull over jacket I was wearing, was covered with blood. This was revealed to me later when I arrived in the hospital. I still could not see because of the burning sensation that I felt earlier from me being sprayed with mace. The officers were unaware of my stabbing suicide attempt from earlier and could not discern where this blood was coming from. I was picked up and put in the back of a squad car while my fleece coat, shirt and under shirt were cut from my body. I was freezing, it was cold outside, and snow was on the ground.

I remember having a conversation with local police officers. I remember telling the officers that I did not kill anyone, and I invited them to my house for coffee. I was later told I had a fluent Spanish conversation with one of their Hispanic officers. The miracle in all of this is that I do not speak or understand Spanish fluently. I was also advised that I spoke three different languages, none of them being English. Shortly after, I passed out in the back seat of the police car and awakened eight hours later in the hospital. Upon my eyes opening, I was greeted by a very sweet, elderly nurse. I called out, "momma is that you?" The nurse responded, "I will be your momma if you want...baby God had His hands on you!" She then raised up a catheter bag and ask, "Do you know what this is?" I responded, "yes." The catheter bag was an opaque white color. Normally they are either clear or slightly yellow from the urine in your bladder. She then said, "This is the second one." This was to imply that the first one looked whiter; like a white sheet of paper.

A doctor came into the room and stood at the foot of the bed. I noticed he was a very sharp dresser, and I told him so. He stated, "I have to dressed this nice because I'm surrounded by women all day." I also noticed he had a perplexed look on his face. The doctor was perplexed because he could not believe why I was alive or how I was even breathing. The doctor then pulled my covers down to check out my two stab wounds in my chest as well as the additional cut I received from the exploratory surgery the doctor had just performed on me. He wanted to make sure the stab wounds I inflicted to myself the night before did not cause any major damage. I was told I was fortunate, because a half an inch deeper I would have pierced my heart

I began to look around the room. I noticed that I was strapped to the bed by my wrists and ankles. I then turned to my left, in the direction of the nurse and began telling her about what I had been experiencing for the past 10 or so hours. The nurse nodded her head, acknowledging what I said and then stated, "you had enough toxins in your body to kill an elephant. We are amazed how you are even here." She then told me, "Rest… there are enemies among you" and nodded her head to my right. As I turned my head to the right I could see several pairs of legs behind a curtain and one police officer sitting along the wall just across from me.

Remembering I had just been in a car accident I thought, "isn't that nice, the officers took me to the hospital and are here to see that I am alright." My thoughts were still somewhat befuddled and they were transitioning from my heaven and hell experience, to my car accident, and now hospital experience. I was having difficulty determining if everything I had experienced was a nightmare, dream or reality. I lay relaxed in my hospital bed, waiting for the food the nurse was about to give me. One nurse gave me a sponge bath and my original nurse began feeding me the food I had ordered and just arrived. I did not know it at the time, but I was severely dehydrated. I had lost 15 plus pounds in less than 5 days and felt extremely tired. The nurse asked me if I needed to use the rest room and I advised her yes. She then turned to one of the officers in the room and asked him if I could be released. The officer, said in a very hostile voice, "Let him crap on himself!" They all began to laugh. Up until that point, there was no conversation between me and the officers. I did not find. their comment amusing at all. The nurse began pleading for me and said, "He is not going to go anywhere, he just had surgery!" I then heard the officer respond, "OK, he can go, but one of us will have to go with him and he has to leave the door open."

I hobbled to the restroom because the officer put shackles on my feet, wrists, and waist. The nurse again, pleaded to have one of my arms unlocked so I could "handle my business." The officer freed my right hand and watched as I used the restroom. How humiliating. At this point I realized something was wrong. I thought, "Maybe the officers are not here for me, but for some other reason?" It still hadn't dawned on me that I had done anything wrong. I walked very slowly back to the bed and got assistance from the nurse as I climbed back in the bed. The wounds in my chest, particularly the new three-inch vertical cut that the surgeon made, was causing me great pain. I was restrained back to the bed and attempted to get some rest.

CHAPTER 6

A RUDE AWAKENING

After a very brief nap, a lady in a long black robe came into my room. The officers stood up and I smiled at her. I was wondering who she was and why she was in my room. The lady introduced herself as being a Judge. One of the officers read me my rights and my arraignment took place in my hospital room, while I was strapped to the bed. I stared in awe as the officer read me my rights. I wondered, "Why are they doing that, what did I do wrong?" Then the judge rattled off seven felony counts and four misdemeanors. I may have been confused, but I fully understood what a felony meant and being sentenced with seven of them was horrendous. My blood pressure immediately shot through the roof. The nurse had to give me a shot in order to bring my blood pressure to a controllable level. I was now being treated like a criminal. My wrist and ankle bed restraints were taken off. I was once again, shackled by my wrists, ankles and waist. I was then carted off to the local county jail. I had never been to jail before except to visit family members and friends. Jail is very different when you are experiencing it from the other side. Due to my medical injury, my surgery on my chest, I was booked through jail through the medical department. This allowed me to have my own room. With me being a first-time jailer, this helped tremendously. Normally I would have entered through what is referred to as the "bull pin". This is a holding area for all arrestees until a cell is prepared for them or one becomes available. The "bull pin" is always over capacity. You are almost literally sleeping on top of one another and if you are fortunate to have a place to lay on the cement floor, you better stay there because you may have to fight in order to get your spot back because now, someone else who had been standing has invaded your spot.

Jail is nothing like you see on television. You don't just call a lawyer and "presto", you are out. Getting out can sometimes be a very long, wasteful, and drawn out process. My experience was being treated like a criminal, "treated" as guilty, until proven innocent, not as how we are taught; you are innocent until proven guilty. You are on the "systems" time, they are not on yours. Most of the inmates are rude, disrespectful and obnoxious. To me, it is the closest experience to hell that you can come to in the natural. I hated being there and did not think I belonged. Time seemed to have slowed to a mere snail's pace, almost a complete stop. I had only been in jail for two days and it seemed like two years. I was a little overjoyed that day because after speaking to my sister, she and my family were going to bond me out of jail the next day, which was Friday. I did not want to have to spend the entire weekend in jail. My sister and wife at the time were going to meet with my lawyer the next day. My lawyer had got the court to issue a $ 25,000 bond for my release. This meant that my family had to come up with 10% or $2,500 to get me out. At the time my family did not have all the $2,500, so I made arrangements with some close friends of mine to give them $2,000 and I would pay them when I got out. Everything was going according to plan. My sister called me and advised me that my friends had given her the money she needed and that she and my wife were going to meet with my lawyer the next day to give him a retainers' fee. I could not believe that in less than 15 hours I would be home, but as usual, satan had another plan, and he was feverishly working to implement it.

On Friday, my sister and wife met with the lawyer and gave him his retainers' fee. My sister headed to the court to pay my bond and my wife headed to work. When my sister arrived at the court, there seemed to be a problem or misunderstanding. Something had gone wrong, something had changed from the time my sister left my lawyers office to the time she reached the courthouse. This was probably less than a 35-minute drive. There was a hold put on my bond and at the time they could not tell my sister why. It would prevent me from being released.

My sister being the blood hound that she is continued to press for answers, time was running out. She wanted to get me out of jail on Friday, but it did not seem like it was going to happen. Around 4:30 pm Friday evening, my sister calls me and informs me that she talked to the district attorney and was told that my wife called and told them that I was getting out of jail and that "she was in fear of her life and the safety of her kids."

This about floored me; I was totally in shock. I am not a violent man, nor have I ever been. I could not believe my wife would say such a thing. I was totally devastated, depressed and violently angry.

Now, I knew I was going to have to stay in jail until Monday and see what would happen. I did not call my wife at all that weekend for fear of what I might say, but mostly in fear of what she might say. I did not want to hear that she in fact called the police and made such a claim. I did not want to hear that she hated me so much that she wanted me locked up. Readers, let me remind you that everything that I am telling you snowballed from the time that I arrived home from my Cancun trip and argued with my wife, less than five days prior. Just six days prior I had experienced both spiritual hell and heaven, and now my life had become a "natural, living hell!"

Friday evening, I was transferred from my one man cell to a 10 man pod. I was put in a cell with all types of people who were being accused of criminal sexual conduct, rape, pedophilia, larceny, arm robbery, embezzlement and aggravated assault. I remember thinking, where is the justice in this. While in my misery and having my own pity party I realized that I too, had committed several crimes, regardless of how they happened, they happened. I had to be held accountable for my actions.

I was very excited when Monday arrived. I thought I would surely be going home today. I was taken to court around 10:30 am. I arrived to the court in shackles that secured my wrists at my waist with my ankles. They were fastened extremely tight and hurt with every movement of my body. As the judge entered everyone in the room was asked to stand. I looked around to court room for family members as I patiently waited for the judge to call me to the stand. Noticing several family members, including my wife and my lawyer made me smile and brought joy to my heart. I was still anxious to know if my wife had actually made that phone call to the district attorney or not?

Finally, I heard, "Darryl Horne, approach the bench." My lawyer and I met up in the center of the court room with the prosecutor and defense attorney to follow. The defense presented its case first. I could not believe some of the things that I was hearing and for a moment I felt as if they had the wrong man on trial. The image of the person they presented to the court definitely was not me. The person that they were trying to make me out to be, I would not even like.

It was our turn to present our case. My lawyer started explaining that I had never been in trouble before, that I was a working man, a father and a college-educated person. He tried to present me as the man that I really was, not the man the prosecuting attorney had conjured up. My family and I were all very worried and nervous. My life was in the decision of this judge and what he decided would determine my future. Finally, my lawyer finished his statements.

The judge briefly looked over the papers in front of him, lifted up his head and stated, "I have heard both parties' argument, bail is set for $1,000,000!" My lawyers' jaw practically fell through the floor, and I almost fainted.

I was nervously crying while wondering how on earth will I come up with that kind of money, I will be in jail for forever. Even the 10% or $100,000 would be impossible. My lawyer began to argue that the bail is excessive, not reasonable and that murderers did not get bails set that high. The judge began to rattle off some more reasons to justify his decision, slammed his gavel done and said, "$1,000,000 and that's final!"

I vigorously cried and lay slump in my chair as the bailiffs approached me to take me back to my new home. I glanced over to see my family in tears as I was led out of the court room. I was taken to the basement and put in a holding cell until I could be later taken back to the county jail. This felt just as bad as hell (Believe me, there is no comparison). Still crying, I pondered, "Why is this happening to me. I'm a good person and I don't understand." Shortly after, a group of inmates along with myself, were driven back to the county jail and escorted back to our cells.

For the next 30 days I was miserable, depressed, angry, scared, confused and most of all, felt betrayed. All of the above mentioned things are of the devil, not of God. The devil still wanted to see me hurt, and still see me in pain. I still could not believe that the women that I loved, my wife, had made one phone call that sent my life into a complete downward spiral. Towards the end of this 30-day trial I decided to call my wife and ask her if she in fact made that call. She told me that she did not. Whether she did or not was not going to change the fact of where I was. I had to forgive her regardless and move on and that is what I chose to do. The first 30 days of being incarcerated were the hardest for me. Seeing everyone in jail and hearing of the circumstances that got them there was very depressing. Some of them seemed, like me, to have been set up. After talking to many of them I noticed that they were not bad people at all. They were in fact good people, just like me, caught up in bad situations. I finally came to the realization I could not fix this, only God could. I also realized I had to let Him fix it on His time, not mine.

I started reading my Bible. For the second time in my life, God was talking to me and again my ears were wide open. It is amazing how God works to our favor to always bring Him glory. I began witnessing to others while in jail. I even started conducting a Bible study right there in the jail cell. In my pod I was nick named "Preacher." God was looking out for me. The pain, hurt, anger, resentment, rage, fear, betrayal and injustice that I was feeling had all been removed by the mercy and grace of our Lord and Savior, Jesus Christ.

I spent the next three months in jails waiting to be heard while patiently waiting for God to implement His plan to get me out; God always has a plan! The judicial system was failing me. My case was being delayed due to court and legal bureaucracy. The process was taking too long. In addition, I was starting to get harassed by some of the guards in the jail due to the nature of my case. Officers do not take too kindly to the fact that you fought or disrespected one of their fellow officers. Even though, this entire nightmare was a misunderstanding, the records stated that I was in jail for assaulting several police officers and that's all they were concerned about. Most of the officers were very respectful and treated me and the rest of the inmates with the same respect we gave them.

One deputy, for some reason, really had it out for me. Too often he would deliberately "shake down" our cell. This is normally prearranged by the sargent, unknowingly to inmates in an attempt to catch them with contraband, illegal things in jail. You would be surprised at some of the things inmates somehow obtain in jail. It is really unbelievable. Late at night while I was sleeping this same deputy would come to my cell and pull the covers off me through the cell bars and leave my cover lying outside the cell. He did this several times per week. This deputy was much younger than I, and I began voicing my opinion. One day I told him, "I was old enough to be his daddy and that he needed to grow up." This only fueled his aggression towards me. The next day he conducted a surprise search of our cell. He asked all of us to go into the empty neighboring cell, which is standard protocol, but this time after completing his search he took all 10 of our personal property boxes and scattered them all over the cell room floor. This may not seem to be that big of a problem to some, but if you have ever been in prison, this can be a huge problem. In prison each inmate is given the opportunity to buy food and personal items that he or she may need from the jail store known as "Commissary." Some of the inmates along with myself, had several boxes of commissary goods. Now, because this deputy wanted to flex his muscles, all of our items were mixed up. If this was done in a prison, a riot could easily erupt because some things are very hard to come by in jail or prison, particularly when you do not have any money.

While we were in the next cell we could hear this deputy literally destroying our belongings. One of the younger inmates who were with us began to get upset and unruly. I went over to the young man, and because of the relationship that I had established with him during our time together I was able to calm him down. Well, apparently this deputy overheard our conversation and did not like some of the things I was saying, because they were pertaining to him. The deputy called me over to the front of the cell where the bars are and as I approached the bars to see what he wanted, he reached in, grabbed me by the shirt and attempted to pull my face into the bars. He then opened the cell and advised us that we could return to our cell. The cell was a mess; I had had enough of jail and this deputy. I immediately called my sister and told her if someone did not get me out I was either going to be badly hurt, or dead. Two days later my other sister got in touch with a bail bondsman, and she put her house up as collateral to get me out. Amen Jesus!

CHAPTER 7

THE DEVIL STILL IS NOT DONE WITH ME

As part of the bond agreement I had to go and stay with my sister. The court had also ordered that I could not go to my house with my wife and kids, nor could I go within 100 yards of my property. If I did I would be held in violation of the court order, charged with that violation and thrown back in jail. Staying away from my house and wife was not going to be that big of a problem, but staying away from my children, and not being an active part of my life was almost a bad as being in hell. My wife and I both had come from very large families. Between our two families, there were a total of 19 siblings. Family was everything to me, but because of my actions that "moment in time", I was now dependent upon someone else in order to see my children. I lived with my sister for roughly four months. During this time, my wife brought the kids by to spend time with me. In all of my mess, seeing them brought comfort to my soul.

During this four-month time frame I also ended up getting sued by two individuals. The driver of the truck that I had crashed into prior to my scuffle with the police, was suing me and one of the police officers who had been injured in the scuffle was suing me.

I was now separated from my wife, with divorce soon approaching. I was glad to be out of jail, but I was greatly saddened that my "family" was slowly being destroyed. I was slowly, trying to put my life back together but was having great difficulties in doing so. My lawyer fees were starting to add up. I was being drawn in and out of court for these two laws suits and being forced to have two doctors visits per week.

I could not drive myself around because, when I crashed into the truck, I totaled my car. I was depending on others to either take me to all of these appointments or use their car and drive myself. I had to attend all of the court hearings, because if I did not, I could be held in contempt and possibly in violation. The last thing I wanted to do was go back to jail. Next to hell, it was the worse experience I ever had. I truly do not understand how people can go back to jail several times or make it a lifetime event. My lawyer fees, expenses and lawsuits exceeded $87,000. I was worried how this was going to get paid and how my seven felonies and four misdemeanors were going to get cleared up. I knew felonies are frowned upon in the work place and if I could not get them removed, I could possibly be terminated or not hired by another employer. I was a nervous wreck. I continued seeing my doctors, lawyers and attended several court hearings for the next several months.

Roughly one and a half years had passed from the time I took those pills until a verdict of not guilty was entered. God had come through for me again. All of the charges were dropped. My slate was completely wiped clean. In addition I was also able to settle my two lawsuits and able to go back to work. God completely repaired all of the damage for me. He will repair your damage too, if you ask. Matthew 7-8 states,

"7 "Ask and it will be given to you; seek and you will find; knock and the door will be opened to you. 8 For everyone who asks receives; the one who seeks finds; and to the one who knocks, the door will be opened."

Luke 11:9-10, "9 "So I say to you: Ask and it will be given to you; seek and you will find; knock and the door will be opened to you. 10 For everyone who asks receives; the one who seeks finds; and to the one who knocks, the door will be opened."

The previous scriptures did not say that God "may"... they say God "will"! God wants to be your provider. God wants to be your Savior. He came into this world for that sole purpose. To sacrifice His life for our sins, so we could spend eternal life with Him. In order for Him to do that, you first and foremost have to want Him to be your God. You have to "ask", "seek", "knock." Ask Him to be your Lord and Savior and I promise you, as he saved me, He will wash away your tears and save you too. Hebrews 10:5-10 states,

"5 Therefore, when Christ came into the world, he said: "Sacrifice and offering you did not desire, but a body you prepared for me; 6 with burnt offerings and sin offerings you were not pleased. 7 Then I said, 'Here I am— it is written about me in the scroll— I have come to do your will, my God.'" 8 First he said, "Sacrifices and offerings, burnt offerings and sin offerings you did not desire, nor were you pleased with them"—though they were offered in accordance with the law. 9 Then he said, "Here I am, I have come to do your will." He sets aside the first to establish the second. 10 And by that will, we have been made holy through the sacrifice of the body of Jesus Christ once for all."

God sacrificed His Son Jesus for the sins of man. The devil tried to separate man from God way back in the Garden of Eden when Adam and Eve allowed themselves to be tempted by Satan and unleashed sin, or the devil into the world. Jesus came to take the sting out of death and to restore us to what is rightfully His, His Kingdom! Jesus truly loves you. The last thing you want to do is die without knowing Jesus. You will find yourself in hell, wondering what in the heck happened and in total disbelief to find out what those "Christians" were telling you about Jesus and the devil were true. I experienced hell, in your wildest dreams you could never experience a taste of what hell is like. It is unreal! God did not make hell for humans. He made hell for the devil and his original flock of angels who rebelled against Christ in Heaven, eons before the earth or humans ever existed. Matthew 23:33 states,

"You snakes! You brood of vipers! How will you escape being condemned to hell?"

Matthew 25: 41, Then he will say to those on his left, 'Depart from me, you who are cursed, into the eternal fire prepared for the devil and his angels."

God does not want one soul to go to hell. Please give your soul to Christ. Get to know Jesus today.

CHAPTER 8

WHY DID I GO TO HELL

I believe I went to hell for several reasons and none of them is because God wanted me to. God allowed it, but believe me, that is not where He wanted me to go. God does not want anyone bad or good, believer or non believer to go to hell. He wants us to give our life over to Him and start living the type of life that He has ordained for us. Please remember, sin is death and death is of the devil, not God. God is Life! When God died on the cross, He took all of our sins with Him, yes, even those that we have yet to commit. As part of His covenant with us, He vowed to sacrifice His life in exchange for ours so we may spend eternal life with Him and the Father. Whenever God exercises a covenant, an agreement or promise, that covenant can never be broken. Even God Himself cannot break it. With every covenant God always provides the conditions that we, as humans and followers of Christ are to abide by. In order for sinners to be redeemed of our sins we have to always do two things. First, we have to accept Christ as our Lord and Savior. Secondly, whenever we commit a sin we have to repent or ask God for forgiveness. When I committed suicide, I murdered myself, both of which are sins. Unfortunately for me, I died in that sin. I did not have time to repent or ask God to forgive me. I was already physically dead. Therefore, spiritually, even though I had accepted Jesus as my Lord and Savior, I was unable to seek repentance before dying. Remember, this was one of the two conditions in order to be saved. At that time, I was only able to exercise one. Secondly just as we have choices to make in life, I too had a choice to make in hell; which master was I going to choose, God or the devil. Who was I going to ask for help or believe was going to redeem me. Matthew 6: 24 states,

"No one can serve two masters. Either you will hate the one and love the other, or you will be devoted to the one and despise the other. You cannot serve both God and money."

Luke 16:13, "No one can serve two masters. Either you will hate the one and love the other, or you will be devoted to the one and despise the other. You cannot serve both God and money."

Exodus 20:3, "You shall have no other gods before me."

Isaiah 44:6, "This is what the LORD says— Israel's King and Redeemer, the LORD Almighty: I am the first and I am the last; apart from me there is no God."

Exodus 34:14, "Do not worship any other god, for the LORD, whose name is Jealous, is a jealous God."

Deuteronomy 4:35, "You were shown these things so that you might know that the LORD is God; besides Him there is no other."

The devil wanted me to denounce Christ, and he wants the same of you. He is a liar, and scriptures say that he is the father of all lies. If I had listened to him, he would have deceived me, just like he deceived Adam and Eve back in the Garden. Instead of sharing this testimony with you, I would be burning in hell right now. My family, friends and loved ones would be mourning my death and the devil would have won. The devil would have won, because he would have succeeded in capturing another soul; one of God's children. Thank you, Jesus! Don't let the devil deceive you.

Another reason why I went to hell was so I could share my experience with as many people who would listen. The Holy Spirit told me, "Don't worry about what they, "the world" will think. Tell those who will listen and let me do the rest. "You plant the seed, and I will water it. You just go and spread the Word!" What Word… the Word of Christ, that hell is real, that Heaven is real and most important, God is real. GOD IS NOT DEAD! He is alive and resides in every one of us.

Lastly, I believe I was sent to hell and then heaven in order for me to fully discern that God is in control. He is the only one who can control life or death. He is the one who determines what happens in our lives. Even if it means allowing the devil to tempt us and in my case being sent to hell. I would not wish this on my worse enemy. I allowed the devil to talk me into killing myself, but the Most High came through once again, but this time with a much better plan. God is ruler over everything. Colossians 1:16-17 states,

"16 For in Him all things were created: things in heaven and on earth, visible and invisible, whether thrones or powers or rulers or authorities; all things have been created through Him and for Him. 17 He is before all things, and in Him all things hold together."

Genesis 14:22, "But Abram said to the king of Sodom, "With raised hand I have sworn an oath to the LORD, God Most High, Creator of heaven and earth."

Genesis 18:25, "Far be it from you to do such a thing—to kill the righteous with the wicked, treating the righteous and the wicked alike. Far be it from you! Will not the Judge of all the earth do right?"

Hebrews 1:3, "The Son is the radiance of God's glory and the exact representation of his being, sustaining all things by his powerful word. After he had provided purification for sins, he sat down at the right hand of the Majesty in heaven."

Daniel 4:17, "The decision is announced by messengers, the holy ones declare the verdict, so that the living may know that the Most High is sovereign over all kingdoms on earth and gives them to anyone he wishes and sets over them the lowliest of people."

Daniel 4:25, "You will be driven away from people and will live with the wild animals; you will eat grass like the ox and be drenched with the dew of heaven. Seven times will pass by for you until you acknowledge that the Most High is sovereign over all kingdoms on earth and gives them to anyone he wishes."

God is trying to let us know that He is the ruler and Lord of Lord's. He has the final say about everything. While in the natural He wants us to make the same choices He would make if He were physically here in the flesh. God wants everyone to become as much like Him as possible, on our own free will before our time is up. When our time has come He will come in and add the final touches that will glorify our bodies and make us exactly like Him and Jesus. What a great blessing! This can only be done by accepting Him as your Lord and Savior.

CHAPTER 9

WHAT DOES THE BIBLE SAY ABOUT HELL AND DEMONS

In the Bible, hell is referenced roughly 154 times. Why do you think that is so? In the biblical Creation found in the book of Genesis, there is no mention made of a place called hell. At Creation, everything that God made was good. However, scripture tells us in Matthew 25:41 that hell was later prepared for "the devil and his angels" (see also Isaiah 14:12). Hell was not created for man; it was never God's intention that any human being, saved or unsaved, good or bad should go to hell. In 2 Peter 3:9, we learn that God does not want "anyone to perish, but everyone to come to repentance." Hell is a real physical place. We know this because it is stated in many verses in the Bible, several of them spoken by Jesus, Himself. We also know that the wicked and unrighteous will go there when they die. Hell is defined many ways:

> *Sheol – the region of departed spirits (Psalm 9:17). Hades – the region of departed spirits of the lost (Matthew 16:18)*

> *Gehenna – a valley of Hinnom where perpetual fires were kept to burn the refuse of Jerusalem. came to be used by Jesus as an appropriate picture of the eternal hell and punishment (Matthew 5:22).*

Tartaroo – the place where those angels is reserved to judgment. The deepest abyss of Hades (2 Peter 2:4).

Limnen tou Puros – (Lake of Fire) the same as the gehenna of fire, the eternal hell and perdition of all spirits (Revelation 19:20).

Matthew 5:22 states, "But I tell you that anyone who is angry with a brother or sister will be subject to judgment."

Again, anyone who says to a brother or sister, 'Raca,' is answerable to the court. And anyone who says, 'You fool!' will be in danger of the fire of hell.

"Matthew 5:29, "If your right eye causes you to stumble, gouge it out and throw it away. It is better for you to lose one part of your body than for your whole body to be thrown into hell."

Matthew 5:30, "And if your right hand causes you to stumble, cut it off and throw it away. It is better for you to lose one part of your body than for your whole body to go into hell."

Matthew 10:28, "Do not be afraid of those who kill the body but cannot kill the soul. Rather, be afraid of the One who can destroy both soul and body in hell."

Matthew 18:9, "And if your eye causes you to stumble, gouge it out and throw it away. It is better for you to enter life with one eye than to have two eyes and be thrown into the fire of hell."

Matthew 23:15, ""Woe to you, teachers of the law and Pharisees, you hypocrites! You travel over land and sea to win a single convert, and when you have succeeded, you make them twice as much a child of hell as you are."

Matthew 23:33, ""You snakes! You brood of vipers! How will you escape being condemned to hell?"

Mark 9:43, "If your hand causes you to stumble, cut it off. It is better for you to enter life maimed than with two hands to go into hell, where the fire never goes out."

Mark 9:45, "And if your foot causes you to stumble, cut it off. It is better for you to enter life The devil's Deception But GOD's Glory! crippled than to have two feet and be thrown into hell."

Mark 9:47, "And if your eye causes you to stumble, pluck it out. It is better for you to enter the kingdom of God with one eye than to have two eyes and be thrown into hell." Hell is identified in both the old and New Testament as a literal place.

Psalm 37:20, "But the wicked will perish: Though the LORD's enemies are like the flowers of the field, they will be consumed, they will go up in smoke."

Malachi 4:1, "Surely the day is coming; it will burn like a furnace. All the arrogant and every evildoer will be stubble, and the day that is coming will set them on fire," says the

LORD Almighty. "Not a root or a branch will be left to them." Matthew 13:42, "They will throw them into the blazing furnace, where there will be weeping and gnashing of teeth."

Luke 16:24, "So he called to Him, 'Father Abraham, have pity on me and send Lazarus to dip the tip of his finger in water and cool my tongue, because I am in agony in this fire.'"

John15:6, "If you do not remain in me, you are like a branch that is thrown away and withers; such branches are picked up, thrown into the fire and burned."

Jude 1:7, "In a similar way, Sodom and Gomorrah and the surrounding towns gave themselves up to sexual immorality and perversion. They serve as an example of those who suffer the punishment of eternal fire."

Revelation 9:2, "When he opened the Abyss, smoke rose from it like the smoke from a gigantic furnace. The sun and sky were darkened by the smoke from the Abyss."

Revelation 14:10, "they, too, will drink the wine of God's fury, which has been poured full strength into the cup of his wrath. They will be tormented with burning sulfur in the presence of the holy angels and of the Lamb."

God's purpose for mankind is to develop holy, righteous character. To make him or her fit to receive the precious gift of eternal life. God created man of the dust of the ground, subject to death, so that if he fails to develop right character he can be released from his misery by death. God has no desire to torment or to torture anyone. God is love (1 John 4:8). He will not condemn anyone because of ignorance, and will ensure that everyone will ultimately learn the truth about His Word and have a real chance for eternal life. But if God granted eternal life to those who continually rebel and refuse to develop righteous character, they would bring misery on themselves as well as others for all eternity!

CHAPTER 10

WHAT DOES THE BIBLE SAY ABOUT ANGELS AND HEAVEN

The word "angel" is derived from the Greek word eggelos, which means "messenger." In Hebrew it means mal'ak. Many times, in the Bible these words are used to reference humans: ordinary people who carry messages (Job 1:14; Luke 7:24; 9:52), priests (Malachi 2:7), church leaders (Rev 1:20), prophets (Isaiah 42:19; Malachi 3:1) .

Sometimes, these names are referenced figuratively of things or events as "messengers": pestilence or plagues (2 Samuel 24:16-17), the pillar of cloud (Exodus 14:19).

Throughout Scripture, they are mainly referenced to describe the whole range of spirits, who were created by God. This includes both good and evil angels, and special categories such as archangel, cherubim, and seraphim. Angels are mentioned at least 108 times in the Old Testament and 165 times in the New Testament.

In Hebrews 1:14, God describes angels as spirits sent to serve the saved. "14 Are not all angels ministering spirits sent to serve those who will inherit salvation?"

Colossians 1:16 states, all angels were created by Jesus. "For by him [Jesus] all things were created: things in heaven and on earth, visible and invisible, whether thrones or powers or rulers or authorities; all things were created by him and for him. "

Angels are powerful spiritual beings. God is just and in His word He says vengeance is His.

2 Thessalonians 1:6-7 states, "6 God is just: He will pay back trouble to those who trouble you 7 and give relief to you who are troubled, and to us as well."

This will happen when the Lord Jesus comes from heaven in blazing fire with his powerful angels. Angels do not marry nor have babies:

Matthew 22:30. "30 At the resurrection people will neither marry nor be given in marriage; they will be like the angels in heaven." Cross references: Matthew 22:30; 24:38

God's angels obey Him and worship Jesus.

Psalm 103:20, "Praise the Lord, you his angels, you mighty ones who do his bidding, who obey his word."

Hebrews 1:6, "And again, when God brings his firstborn into the world, he says, "Let all God's angels worship him." God's angels praise Him and refuse to receive worship.

Psalm 148:2, "Praise him, all his angels; praise him, all his heavenly hosts."

Revelations 19: 9-10, and Revelations 22: 8-9.

"9 Then the angel said to me, "Write this: Blessed are those who are invited to the wedding supper of the Lamb!" And he added, "These are the true words of God."10 At this I fell at his feet to worship him. But he said to me, "Don't do that! I am a fellow servant with you and with your brothers and sisters who hold to the testimony of Jesus. Worship God! For it is the Spirit of prophecy who bears testimony to Jesus."

"8 I, John, am the one who heard and saw these things. And when I had heard and seen them, I fell down to worship at the feet of the angel who had been showing them to me. 9 But he said to me, "Don't do that! I am a fellow servant with you and with your fellow prophets and with all who keep the words of this scroll. Worship God!"

When Jesus was tempted by the devil and arose from the grave He was attended by angels.

Matthew 4:11, "Then the devil left him, and angels came and attended him."

Matthew 26:53, "Do you think I cannot call on my Father, and he will at once put at my disposal more than twelve legions of angels?"

John 20:11-12, "Now Mary stood outside the tomb crying. As she wept, she bent over to look into the tomb 12 and saw two angels in white, seated where Jesus' body had been, one at the head and the other at the foot."

Angels are sent to earth to guard and protect the righteous, bring deliverance and execute judgment.

Psalm 91:11, "For he will command his angels concerning you to guard you in all your ways."

Daniel 6:22, "My God sent his angel, and he shut the mouths of the lions. They have not hurt me, because I was found innocent in his sight. Nor have I ever done any wrong before you, Your Majesty."

Acts 5:19, "But during the night an angel of the Lord opened the doors of the jail and brought them out."

Psalm 78:49, "He unleashed against them his hot anger, his wrath, indignation and hostility—a band of destroying angels."

Angels will be used to find everything on or in the earth that causes sin and seek out the unsaved.

Matthew 13:41, "The Son of Man will send out his angels, and they will weed out of his kingdom everything that causes sin and all who do evil." Angels will throw the unsaved into the fiery furnace called "Hell".

Matthew 13:49-50, "49 This is how it will be at the end of the age. The angels will come and separate the wicked from the righteous 50 and throw them into the blazing furnace, where there will be weeping and gnashing of teeth."

Upon the return of Jesus, He will bring a multitude of angels with Him and will reward His saints according to how well they carried out Gods will while on earth.

Matthew 16:27, "For the Son of Man is going to come in his Father's glory with his angels, and then he will reward each person according to what they have done.

When the rapture takes place, angels will gather the righteous and take them to their home in the afterlife.

Matthew 24:31, "And he will send his angels with a loud trumpet call, and they will gather his elect from the four winds, from one end of the heavens to the other."

Mark 13:27, "And he will send his angels and gather his elect from the four winds, from the ends of the earth to the ends of the heavens."

Luke 16:22, "The time came when the beggar died and the angels carried him to Abraham's side. The rich man also died and was buried."

Angels observe servants of God:

1 Corinthians 4:9, "For it seems to me that God has put us apostles on display at the end of the procession, like those condemned to die in the arena. We have been made a spectacle to the whole universe, to angels as well as to human beings."

In the end times, angels will be judged by Christians.

1 Corinthians 6:3, "Do you not now that we will judge angels? How much more the things of this life!"

Angels are real folks, now let me tell you where we and they came from, Heaven. According to scripture, Heaven is a real and physical place. Scripture also tells us that God made heaven and that is where He has His throne.

Genesis 1:1 states, "In the beginning God created the heavens and the earth."

1 Chronicles 29:11 says that everything in heaven and on earth belongs to the Lord:

"Yours, Lord, is the greatness and the power and the glory and the majesty and the splendor, for everything in heaven and earth is yours. Yours, Lord, is the kingdom; you are exalted as head over all."

2 Chronicles 7:14 tells us that God listens to us from Heaven:

"if my people, who are called by my name, will humble themselves and pray and seek my face and turn from their wicked ways, then I will hear from heaven, and I will forgive their sin and will heal their land."

In Matthew 23:9, Jesus Christ told us that the Father lives in heaven:

"And do not call anyone on earth 'father,' for you have one Father, and he is in heaven."

Ecclesiastes 5:2 again shows us that God is in Heaven and that He should be treated with the utmost respect:

"Do not be quick with your mouth, do not be hasty in your heart to utter anything before God. God is in heaven and you are on earth, so let your words be few."

Throughout scripture God is often referred to as the "God of heaven". For example, Nehemiah 1:5 says:

"Then I said: "Lord, the God of heaven, the great and awesome God, who keeps his covenant of love with those who love him and keep his commandments"."

Psalm 103:19 tells us that God's throne is in heaven:

"The Lord has established his throne in heaven, and his kingdom rules over all."

This being said scripture also states God is so big that heaven cannot contain Him.

Jeremiah 23:24, "Who can hide in secret places so that I cannot see them?" declares the Lord. "Do not I fill heaven and earth?" declares the Lord."

God looks down from heaven, watches what we are doing, and sees who is listening to Him.

Psalm 14:2, "The Lord looks down from heaven on all mankind to see if there are any who understand, any who seek God."

In Matthew 4:17, Jesus declared He was setting up the kingdom of heaven:

"From that time on Jesus began to preach, "Repent, for the kingdom of heaven has come near."

Matthew 5:19 states those who break God's commandments will be called the least in heaven:

"Therefore anyone who sets aside one of the least of these commands and teaches others accordingly will be called least in the kingdom of heaven, but whoever practices and teaches these commands will be called great in the kingdom of heaven."

In Matthew 6:9 Jesus teaches us to pray to God the Father as "Our Father in heaven":

"This, then, is how you should pray: "Our Father in heaven, hallowed be your name."

According to Matthew 5:11-12 all Christians will be rewarded in heaven:

"11Blessed are you when people insult you, persecute you and falsely say all kinds of evil against you because of me. 12 Rejoice and be glad, because great is your reward in heaven, for in the same way they persecuted the prophets who were before you."

In fact, Jesus instructs us to store up treasures in heaven:

Matthew 6.19-21, "19Do not store up for yourselves treasures on earth, where moths and vermin destroy, and where thieves break in and steal. 20 But store up for yourselves treasures in heaven, where moths and vermin do not destroy, and where thieves do not break in and steal. 21 For where your treasure is, there your heart will be also."

In Matthew 10:32, Jesus says that He will acknowledge those in heaven who acknowledge Him on earth:

"Whoever acknowledges me before others, I will also acknowledge before my Father in heaven."

According to Luke 15:7, every time a sinner repents and gives his or her life to Christ there is rejoicing in heaven:

"I tell you that in the same way there will be more rejoicing in heaven over one sinner who repents than over ninety-nine righteous persons who do not need to repent."

In John 6:38, Jesus tells us that He came from heaven specifically to do God's will and in Acts 1:11 that after He died on the cross and rose from the dead He ascended into heaven.

"38For I have come down from heaven not to do my will but to do the will of him who sent me."

"11Men of Galilee," they said, "why do you stand here looking into the sky? This same Jesus, who has been taken from you into heaven, will come back in the same way you have seen him go into heaven."

Jesus is right now in heaven at the right hand of God the Father according to Acts 7:55:

"But Stephen, full of the Holy Spirit, looked up to heaven and saw the glory of God, and Jesus standing at the right hand of God."

In addition, heaven is the final destination for all of those who believe in Christ:

2 Corinthians 5:1, "For we know that if the earthly tent we live in is destroyed, we have a building from God, an eternal house in heaven, not built by human hands."

Philippians 3:20 tells us that believer's citizenship is in heaven and Revelations 19:11-14 proclaims that one day the Lord will return from heaven along with His army to judge and destroy the earth:

"20 But our citizenship is in heaven. And we eagerly await a Savior from there, the Lord Jesus Christ."

"11 I saw heaven standing open and there before me was a white horse, whose rider is called Faithful and True. With justice he judges and wages war. 12 His eyes are like blazing fire, and on his head are many crowns. He has a name written on him that no one knows but he himself. 13 He is dressed in a robe dipped in blood, and his name is the Word of God. 14 The armies of heaven were following him, riding on white horses and dressed in fine linen, white and clean."

Daniel 12:2-3 explains that those who have worked to lead others to Christ will receive great rewards in heaven:

"2 Multitudes who sleep in the dust of the earth will awake: some to everlasting life, others to shame and everlasting contempt. 3 Those who are wise will shine like the brightness of the heavens, and those who lead many to righteousness, like the stars for ever and ever."

According to Revelation 21:2-3, all those who belong to Jesus or who are believers will be part of the new heaven and new earth:

"2 I saw the Holy City, the new Jerusalem, coming down out of heaven from God, prepared as a bride beautifully dressed for her husband. 3 And I heard a loud voice from the throne saying, "Look! God's dwelling place is now among the people, and he will dwell with them. They will be his people, and God himself will be with them and be their God.""

According to John 6:44, Acts 4:12 and Acts 16:30-31, there is only one Way to enter heaven and that is through Jesus Christ:

"44No one can come to me unless the Father who sent me draws them, and I will raise them up at the last day."

"12 Salvation is found in no one else, for there is no other name under heaven given to mankind by which we must be saved."

"30 He then brought them out and asked, "Sirs, what must I do to be saved?" 31 They replied, "Believe

in the Lord Jesus, and you will be saved—you and your household.""

Jesus is our salvation. He is the only way! Those who either don't believe in Jesus or just don't want to give up their sinful ways and reject the holy spirit and God's guidance will end up in hell because of not choosing Him. Revelations 21:7-8 shows the fate of those not going to heaven:

"7Those who are victorious will inherit all this, and I will be their God and they will be my children.8 But the cowardly, the unbelieving, the vile, the murderers, the sexually immoral, those who practice magic arts, the idolaters and all liars—they will be consigned to the fiery lake of burning sulfur. This is the second death."

I have been to hell and it is no place for anyone. I personally would not even want the devil and or his demons to go there…it is just that torturous; pain beyond your wildest imagination! According to Matthew 25:41 hell was made for the devil and his angels (demons), not humans,

"Then he will say to those on his left, 'Depart from me, you who are cursed, into the eternal fire prepared for the devil and his angels. Cross references: Matthew 7:23; Isaiah 66:24; Matthew 3:12; Mark 9:43,48; Luke 3:17; Jude 7; 2 Peter 2:4

Luke 16:14-31 and John 11:1-43 talks of the story of the rich man and Lazarus. The rich man who died without accepting Christ is forever denied access to heaven and God. It is an eternal location from which no one can depart. I hope and pray that no one ever goes there. Jesus is the only way to heaven. Jesus Christ died after living a perfect life. He gave His blood as a sacrifice so that the Holy Father's wrath for us would come upon Himself. He bridged the gap from hell to heaven. His salvation is a free gift to us from God; to reject His salvation is to seal your fate forever. To accept His salvation is to be with God in heaven for eternity in joyful bliss. If you ask Jesus Christ to be your Savior, ask Him to forgive your sins, admit you are a sinner in need of saving, and place your faith and trust in Him, He promises never to forsake you. He will keep you in His own hand and never cast you away, even when you die:

John 6:37, 10:28-29: "37 All those the Father gives me will come to me, and whoever comes to me I will never drive away."

"28 I give them eternal life, and they shall never perish; no one will snatch them out of my hand. 29 My Father, who has given them to me, is greater than all; no one can snatch them out of my Father's hand."

If you do this right now you will see heaven for yourself. You will be with the Lord our God forever and ever when you leave this earth. Those who accept Jesus will inherit the Kingdom of God and Jesus Christ will be our Lord. God wants this for everyone and so do I, and for this reason in the following chapter, I explain why I am led to share my testimony.

CHAPTER 11

WHY I AM LED TO SHARE MY TESTIMONY WITH YOU

The Holy Spirit has led me to share my testimony because there are many lost loved ones. Individuals who are going through tough times and feel there is no way out. I am here to tell you that Jesus is the only way.

He will solve all of your needs, all of your cares, and wipe away all your tears and pain. If He will go to the depths of hell to save me, He will do the same for you. He will not ask you if He can save you. You have to want and choose to be saved. Luke 19:10 states:

"For the Son of Man came to seek and to save the lost."

Jesus does not want to condemn or punish you. He wants to heal and save you.

Most individuals who do not turn to Christ either do not believe in Him, have lost faith due to hardships of life and some because they have done so much evil, they do not feel anyone can cleanse them, not even God. God loves us so much that once we give our life back to Him and accept Him as our Lord and Savior, He does not even remember the sin that we committed while catering to the devil and living in sin.

Hebrews 8:12, "For I will be merciful to their unrighteousness, and their sins and their iniquities will I remember no more."

Hebrews 10:17, "And their sins and iniquities will I remember no more."

Isaiah 43:25, "I, even I, am He that blots out your transgressions for My own sake, and will not remember your sins."

Jeremiah 31:34, "For I will forgive their iniquity, and I will remember their sin no more."

God loves you; He loves you very much, so much that He created His Son Jesus Christ solely for the purpose of being a sacrificial lamb for the forgiveness of our sins.

John 3:16, "For God so loved the world that he gave his one and only Son, that whoever believes in him shall not perish but have eternal life."

The devil wants you to think God does not exist or wants you not to believe in Him. The devil is totally diametrically opposite of God. God is good; therefore the devil is bad.

God is light; therefore, the devil is dark. God is love, merciful and kind, therefore the devil is hateful, merciless and evil. The devil is a liar and the deceiver of the world.

Revelation 12:9, "The great dragon was hurled down—that ancient serpent called the devil, or Satan, who leads the whole world astray. He was hurled to the earth, and his angels with him."

2 John 1:7, "I say this because many deceivers, who do not acknowledge Jesus Christ as coming in the flesh, have gone out into the world. Any such person is the deceiver and the antichrist."

God is Love. Several scriptures show what and how God's love is.

1 John 4:8, "Whoever does not love does not know God, because God is love."

Genesis 20:13, "And when God had me wander from my father's household, I said to her, 'This is how you can show your love to me: Everywhere we go, say of me, "He is my brother."'"

Genesis 22:2, "Then God said, "Take your son, your only son, whom you love—Isaac—and go to the region of Moriah. Sacrifice him there as a burnt offering on a mountain I will show you.""

In Genesis 22:5-8, why did God ask Isaac to sacrifice his son? He did it not to punish him but to increase his faith and to prepare him for His next purpose. He wanted Abraham to have complete (the Ultimate) faith in Him, no matter what the circumstance or situation looked like.

Deuteronomy 7:9, "Know therefore that the Lord your God is God; he is the faithful God, keeping his covenant of love to a thousand generations of those who love him and keep his commandments."

Deuteronomy 10:12, "[Fear the Lord] And now, Israel, what does the Lord your God ask of you but to fear the Lord your God, to walk in obedience to him, to love him, to serve the Lord your God with all your heart and with all your soul."

Deuteronomy 13:3, "you must not listen to the words of that prophet or dreamer. The Lord your God is testing you to find out whether you love him with all your heart and with all your soul.

Deuteronomy 30:20, "and that you may love the Lord your God, listen to his voice, and hold fast to him. For the Lord is your life, and he will give you many years in the land he swore to give to your fathers, Abraham, Isaac and Jacob."

1 Kings 8:23, "and said: "Lord, the God of Israel, there is no God like you in heaven above or on earth below—you who keep your covenant of love with your servants who continue wholeheartedly in your way."

1 Kings 10:9, "Praise be to the Lord your God, who has delighted in you and placed you on the throne of Israel. Because of the Lord's eternal love for Israel, he has made you king to maintain justice and righteousness."

1 Kings 11:2,"They were from nations about which the Lord had told the Israelites, "You must not intermarry with them, because they will surely turn your hearts after their gods." Nevertheless, Solomon held fast to them in love."

2 Chronicles 6:14, "He said: "Lord, the God of Israel, there is no God like you in heaven or on earth— you who keep your covenant of love with your servants who continue wholeheartedly in your way."

2 Chronicles 9:8, "Praise be to the Lord your God, who has delighted in you and placed you on his throne as king to rule for the Lord your God. Because of the love of your God for Israel and his desire to uphold them forever, he has made you king over them, to maintain justice and righteousness.""

Nehemiah 13:26, "Was it not because of marriages like these that Solomon king of Israel sinned? Among the many nations there was no king like him. He was Loved by his God, and God made him king over all Israel, but even he was led into sin by foreign women."

Psalm 36:7, "How priceless is your unfailing love, O God! People take refuge in the shadow of your wings."

Psalm 42:8, "By day the Lord directs his love, at night his song is with me— a prayer to the God of my life."

Psalm 98:3, "He has remembered his love and his faithfulness to Israel; all the ends of the earth have seen the salvation of our God."

Ecclesiastes 9:9, "Enjoy life with your wife, whom you love, all the days of this meaningless life that God has given you under the sun—all your meaningless days. For this is your lot in life and in your toilsome labor under the sun."

Jeremiah 32:18, "You show love to thousands but bring the punishment for the parents' sins into the laps of their children after them. Great and mighty God, whose name is the Lord Almighty."

Hosea 3:1, "The Lord said to me, "Go, show your love to your wife again, though she is loved by another man and is an adulteress. Love her as the Lord loves the Israelites, though they turn to other gods and love the sacred raisin cakes.""

Hosea 4:1, "Hear the word of the Lord, you Israelites, because the Lord has a charge to bring against you who live in the land: "There is no faithfulness, no love, no acknowledgment of God in the land."

Hosea 9:1, "Do not rejoice, Israel; do not be jubilant like the other nations. For you have been unfaithful to your God; you love the wages of a prostitute at every threshing floor.

Hosea 11:1, "[God's Love for Israel] "When Israel was a child, I loved him, and out of Egypt I called my son."

Joel 2:13, "Rend your heart and not your garments. Return to the Lord your God, for he is gracious and compassionate, slow to anger and abounding in love, and he relents from sending calamity."

Jonah 4:2, "He prayed to the Lord, "Isn't this what I said, Lord, when I was still at home? That is what I tried to forestall by fleeing to Tarshish. I knew that you are a gracious and compassionate God, slow to anger and abounding in love, a God who relents from sending calamity.

Michah 6:8, "He has shown you, O mortal, what is good. And what does the Lord require of you? To act justly and to love mercy and to walk humbly with your God."

Zephaniah 3:17, "The Lord your God is with you, the Mighty Warrior who saves. He will take great delight in you; in his love he will no longer rebuke you, but will rejoice over you with singing.""

Malachi 1:2, "I have loved you," says the Lord. "But you ask, 'How have you loved us?' "Was not Esau Jacob's brother?" declares the Lord. "Yet I have loved Jacob."

Malachi 2:11, "Judah has been unfaithful. A detestable thing has been committed in Israel and in Jerusalem: Judah has desecrated the sanctuary the Lord loves by marrying women who worship a foreign god.

Romans 8:39, "neither height nor depth, nor anything else in all creation, will be able to separate us from the love of God that is in Christ Jesus our Lord."

1 Corinthians 2:9, "However, as it is written: "What no eye has seen, what no ear has heard, and what no human mind has conceived"— the things God has prepared for those who love him."

1 Corinthians 8:3, "But whoever loves God is known by God." Ephesians 2:4, "But because of his great love for us, God, who is rich in mercy."

Colossians 2:2, "My goal is that they may be encouraged in heart and united in love, so that they may have the full riches of complete understanding, in order that they may know the mystery of God, namely, Christ."

2 Thessalonians 1:3, " We ought always to thank God for you, brothers and sisters, and rightly so, because your faith is growing more and more, and the love all of you have for one another is increasing."

Hebrews 6:10, "God is not unjust; he will not forget your work and the love you have shown him as you have helped his people and continue to help them."

2 Peter 1:17, "He received honor and glory from God the Father when the voice came to him from the Majestic Glory, saying, "This is my Son, whom I love; with him I am well pleased.""

1 John 2:5, "But if anyone obeys his word, love for God is truly made complete in them. This is how we know we are in him."

1 John 3:1, "See what great love the Father has lavished on us, that we should be called children of God! And that is what we are! The reason the world does not know us is that it did not know him."

1 John 3:10, "This is how we know who the children of God are and who the children of the devil are: Anyone who does not do what is right is not God's child, nor is anyone who does not love their brother and sister."

1 John 4:8, "Whoever does not love does not know God, because God is love."

1 John 4:9, "This is how God showed his love among us: He sent his one and only Son into the world that we might live through him."

1 John 4:10, "This is love: not that we loved God, but that he loved us and sent his Son as an atoning sacrifice for our sins."

1 John 4:12, "No one has ever seen God; but if we love one another, God lives in us and his love is made complete in us."

1 John 4:16, "And so we know and rely on the love God has for us. God is love. Whoever lives in love lives in God, and God in them."

1 John 4:20, "Whoever claims to love God yet hates a brother or sister is a liar. For whoever does not love their brother and sister, whom they have seen, cannot love God, whom they have not seen."

1 John 5:1, "Everyone who believes that Jesus is the Christ is born of God, and everyone who loves the father loves his child as well."

1 John 5:2, "This is how we know that we love the children of God: by loving God and carrying out his commands."

1 John 5:3, "In fact, this is love for God: to keep his commands. And his commands are not burdensome.

In Chapter 1, I stated that God told me I did not know Him. I knew of Him but, He was right, I did not know Him. If I did, I would have never tried to kill myself nor allowed the devil to push me to the point of suicide. If you have never experienced God's love or don't know Him as Love, then you don't know God either. Let me help you get to know Him. One day every knee will bow whether you believe or not. Life is everlasting when you accept Christ. So too is death when you chose to reject His love. Chose Christ and live forever. God is good, His mercy is everlasting and His truth endures forever.

God will never allow anyone to be tempted beyond what they can handle.

1 Corinthians 10:13, "No temptation has overtaken you except what is common to mankind. And God is faithful; he will not let you be tempted beyond what you can bear. But when you are tempted, he will also provide a way out so that you can endure it."

If you are experiencing difficult times it is because you are more than likely conforming to the world or acting outside the will of God. God wants us to act according to His will not our own.

Romans 12:2, "2 Do not conform to the pattern of this world, but be transformed by the renewing of your mind. Then you will be able to test and approve what God's will is—his good, pleasing and perfect will."

We should always trust in the Lord and look to His understanding.

Proverbs 3:5-6 states, "5 Trust in the Lord with all your heart and lean not on your own understanding; 6 in all your ways submit to him, and he will make your paths straight."

Jeremiah 29:11 declares that God has a plan for each and every one of us:

"For I know the plans I have for you," declares the Lord, "plans to prosper you and not to harm you, plans to give you hope and a future."

Proverbs 16:9, "9 In their hearts humans plan their course, but the Lord establishes their steps."

You never go wrong when you allow Jesus to walk for you. God has great things in store for those who love Him and He is just overjoyed to give to those who believe. Please trust God, believe and receive.

1 Corinthians 2:9, "However, as it is written: "What no eye has seen, what no ear has heard, and what no human mind has conceived"— the things God has prepared for those who love him."

CHAPTER 12

WHAT YOU NEED TO DO TO BE SAVED AND GO TO HEAVEN

Jesus Christ is the answer! Sin entered into the world through one man and that one man is Adam who is introduced to the world in Genesis.

Romans 5:12 states "therefore, just as sin entered the world through one man, and death through sin, and in this way death came to all people, because all sinned…"

God gave Adam a commandment to not eat of the tree of the knowledge of good and evil for the day that you do, you shall surely die.

Genesis 2:9 "The Lord God made all kinds of trees grow out of the ground—trees that were pleasing to the eye and good for food. In the middle of the garden were the tree of life and the tree of the knowledge of good and evil."

Genesis 2:17, "but you must not eat from the tree of the knowledge of good and evil, for when you eat from it you will certainly die."

When Adam disobeyed God, everyone born thereafter automatically inherited a sinful nature, and the wages associated with it, which is death. This was a major problem because Adam is the father of all humans. Now, being like God and Jesus, and now having a sinful and Godly nature, sin would live forever as stated in Genesis 3:22:

"And the Lord God said, "The man has now become like one of us, knowing good and evil. He must not be allowed to reach out his hand and take also from the tree of life and eat and live forever."

God provided a solution for that problem, and that solution is Christ! This solution is confirmed and provided in John 3:16:

"For God so loved the world that He gave His only begotten son, that who so ever believeth in Him shall not perish but have everlasting life".

Upon accepting Jesus as your Lord and Savior you become the "whosoever." You cannot work for or earn salvation. God graciously presented man His son Jesus as a free gift and sacrifice to atone man of all sin.

Ephesians 2:8-9 states, "8 For it is by grace you have been saved, through faith—and this is not from yourselves, it is the gift of God— 9 not by works, so that no one can boast".

As a born-again believer, you have acquired the right to receive God's gift and become part of His family as reflected in John 1:12:

"Yet to all who did receive him, to those who believed in his name, he gave the right to become children of God."

If you are willing and ready to chose life through Jesus Christ and be welcomed into His family, I enthusiastically honor you for reciting this prayer:

"I believe Jesus is the Son of God. I believe He died personally for me on the cross and took all of my sins upon Him. I believe He rose from the dead and is currently seated at the right hand of the Father in heaven. Dear Father God, come into my heart and life right now! In my heart I do believe. In my heart I do receive. Therefore, I speak open heartedly that Jesus is my personal Lord and Savior. Thank you, Lord, for receiving me and I am born again right now!"

AMEN and hallelujah…Welcome to the Kingdom of GOD!!!

So that your new walk in Christ can be nourished and you can stay connected, please feel free to get additional information and guidance from divinepreventionministries. org. or a local Holy Spirit bible led church.

If you are looking for a church home or have a prayer request, please reach out via the above web address or contact your local church. Someone will follow up with you once the request has been received. I would like to personally thank you and look forward to our walk together through Christ.

Closing remarks to my readers

I didn't know Him (Jesus)– I was a self-made man. I had a career, cars, money, a family, owned property, travelled. I earned three degrees and was working on my PhD. I was living the good life and all by my hands. I was singing my own praises. A gradual change was coming, but I wasn't worried. I fixed other people's problems; surely, I could fix my own. I was that guy. Slowly my life was turning into a living hell. I lost everything. My home, my job, my properties and what I loved most – my wife. The enemy was winning as I gave in to the attack on my life. Suicide was my fix. Pills, guns, stabbing – all self-inflicted. In my last breaths I called out to God with the only scripture I could remember, Psalm 100. God told me that I read 100's of books but never His. He said, "You Don't Know Me". Miraculously, He brought me back from what the enemy had planned as my death. I rededicated my life to God. I've read his book from cover to cover multiple times and now make it an annual event. I'm living my life according to His word like never before. Now, I have my life and my wife back. All to the glory of God!

Testimonies of God's GLORY

Melissa Thompson Whitsett

In August 2010 I was informed that I had a pancreatic tumorthatwasgrowingandwiththistypeofcancerthere is no cure. I was advised that the doctors were going to remove the tumor and if it was cancerous there was a possibility that it could metastasize and spread throughout my body. Upon opening me up the doctors could no longer find the tumor, the tumor was gone. The doctors did notice that my gull bladder was enlarged. When I found out all of this I cried out to God, I said "I have not even lived yet." I had just started to live my life. I had just got a divorce after experiencing a horrible marriage. My oldest daughter was in college, my other daughter and oldest son were in high school and my youngest son was just four years old. I was a single mom and I was devastated at the thought that I could die and I would have to leave my family. I had a "why me" moment and I could not believe that I might be leaving my children at such a young age. I began to pray to God and I told Him that I know His hand has been on my life for many years and He has never failed me, and I know you won't fail me now. I had many people praying for me, my family and my whole church was praying for me. That is when the doctors told me that the tumor was gone. All that was left was just some fatty tissue.

Even though the tumor was gone I began to have complications from the surgery. Two days after my surgery the whole left side of my body was swollen. I was in excruciating pain. When I went in the hospital, I weighed 150 lbs. and within two days I weighed 202 lbs., I gained 52 lbs. of water. This led me to congestive heart failure. Fluid was filling my lungs, and I was suffocating. I could barely breathe and could not talk. It felt like something was pressing on my chest and preventing me from breathing. The doctors said I developed interstitial lung disease, which is a swelling of the lungs and causes shortness of breath. The doctors said I would have this for the rest of my life.

During my hospital stay I coded twice, had a heart attack and went into respiratory distress. I spent the next seven days in ICU hooked up to a vent. My condition had gotten so bad the doctors had to put me in a medically induced coma. I had a third heart attack while on the vent and the doctors told my family that I was going to die, to prepare for the worse. I could not breathe at all on my own, the machine they had me hooked up to do the breathing for me.

No one gave up on me and many prayed to God. The doctor put me on a very high dose of steroids which caused the fluid in my lungs to go away and the swelling to go down. My hospital stay was only supposed to be four days and ended up being 2 ½ months. While in my coma I had many dreams and visions. I dreamt my bed was in my sisters' living room, and I could see many family members walking around me talking. I felt peace and quiet in the room. I had another dream that took me back to my teenage years when I first accepted Christ as my Lord and

Savior. I was in a room in the basement of the house we lived in at the time. The room was powder blue. I used to sneak in this room and pray. Whenever I went into this room God's presence would also enter into the room. It was very hot in this room when God's presence was with me. When I was in the coma God took me to this room because that is where I felt safe and comfortable. As a teen this blue room was like my prayer room. God also took me to another place, I don't know where, but it was white all around me. I was kneeling in front of God and I could feel Him covering me, as if to comfort me. He was letting me know that He was there and that I was safe. This whole experience has taught me that God is my protector, comforter, and that He cares about me, loves me, and no matter where I am at He is always there and will never forsake me just like His word says.

Shalida Minter

While growing to maturity, I have made several suicide attempts; around eight of them. All of my suicide attempts have been done by me taking pills. My first attempt was when I was nine years old. As a kid, I was often embarrassed in public by my mom. I always felt like that kid who did not belong in that family. My opinions did not matter, and no one cared what I thought or what I had to say. My mother was verbally, physically, and emotionally abusive. As far as religion goes, I was very confused. My parents were Muslim. The way my parents taught Islam was different. There were different kinds of rules and a very hostile environment. We were not allowed to say Jesus Christ and if I got caught sneaking to church or singing a church song I got beaten or punished. Jesus Christ and or Christianity were not allowed in the house. Therefore during my childhood, I felt like I did not belong and I thought if I had to live like this on this planet I would rather be gone. I ingested a bunch of Tylenol. The Tylenol made me sick and I began vomiting a lot. I had gotten so sick that I had to tell my mother what I had done. The sickness and discomfort was unbearable. I was taken to the hospital and had my stomach pumped free of the pills.

Throughout my life I had various bouts with depression. I dealt with the depression the easiest and only way I knew how, by taking pills in an attempt to die. I felt the only answer to my problems were to kill myself and that way I would never have to deal with it anymore. But, no matter how many attempts that I made, I always woke up, most of the time disappointed that I did not succeed. After so many suicide attempts I was eventually admitted into the hospital where, instead of being helped, I was talked about, stigmatized and scrutinized by the doctors and family. I never got to the root of my problems.

What I have realized in my adult life, particularly in the last three years, is that I was not a strong person. I believed in God but my faith was weak. During stressful times instead on calling on Him I would panic. When I lost my job a few years ago, I had to turn to God. I was making good money working in the hospital, and then things instantly changed and I was fired. I was scared and instead of crying, curling up in a ball or confining myself to my room, I called on Jesus. Losing my job was actually a blessing to me. I worked a job that I did not like just to try to make ends meet. Even though I did not like what I was doing, I always made sure I did a good job. I did not have a place to live. I often cried out to God and asked Him to help me and help me understand what was going on. I think God was humbling me and strengthening my faith while showing me His love. He got me the apartment I currently live in. I could not pay the monthly rent amount or the security deposit. I was able to get the apartment by His grace through the apartment owners. For some reason, the owners liked me and showed me favor. They worked with me and accepted what I could pay until I was able to pay the full monthly rent amount.

While growing up I was always dependent upon my mother and my sister and I always looked to them for advice and counseling. In the past I usually lived with both or one of them. The Lord began showing and teaching me to believe in Him when I was able to move out on my own for the first time in my life. God was showing me that I could be independent of others but totally dependent on Him. I did not know it at the time though.

I used to always put others up on pedestals and I should have been putting God there. I was worshiping my mother, my sister, my friends and my family. Everyone but God… He revealed to me that this is not the way it is suppose to be. I was not to put anyone or anything before Him. It took a lot for me to understand this. When I first lost my job four years ago the ones I depended upon the most just stopped speaking to me. My mother, sister and friends were all gone. All I felt I had was my daughter and by the grace of God my landlord. I got my apartment in 2009. The irony in this is that the listing for the apartment was in April, I inquired about the apartment in August of 2008. The apartment should have been gone. I called the number on the advertisement and talked with the landlord who lived in Florida. I was advised that someone had just moved out of an apartment. I went and looked at it and my daughter and I moved in. The Glory in this is that I explained to the landlord that I lost my job and did not currently have one. The landlord still let me get the place. Glory to God!

At that time my sister was also going through challenges of her own which is why she and I had not talked. My landlord advised me that she would work with me until I got back on my feet. She told me to pay whatever I could and if I could not pay rent for the month just to let her know. My landlords were Christian. God sent these angels to me to help build me up, my faith up and draw me closer to Him. At that time an unbelievable calm came upon me even though my best friend had just died. My friend taught me how to forgive, forget, and keep our personal business personal, you don't just share your business with everyone. Everything happens for a reason. God was preparing me for the now, because the person that I am today and who I was four years ago are totally different. I don't cry, I don't worry and I know God is my provider.

A few years ago, I was at my lowest point in my life. I had lost my job, my best friend had died, my daughter was pregnant, I did not have a place to live and felt I had no one to turn to. I was once again depressed and I did not want to deal with life and I went back to my easy out, suicide. I crushed up 60 pills and ingested them while drinking a bottle of wine. In my previous suicide attempts I did not care about life but for some reason, this time I did. I realized I had made a mistake but didn't know what to do about it. I began to pray. I never prayed so hard in my life. Earlier in the year I met a lady who was pastoring a church. I called her and asked her to come over to my house. I did not tell her what I had done. When she arrived, she blessed my house and baptized me in the bathtub. By this time the pills had been in my system about 20 hours. I had not slept yet, I was afraid to fall to sleep in fear of not waking up. I could feel my insides tightening up from the pills affecting my body, but I did not tell her. After she baptized me and left, I went in the bedroom, got in the bed and fell asleep. I fell in a deep, deep sleep for 20 hours. While I was sleep I saw bright lights all around me and I could hear the lights buzzing all around me. These lights were passing up and down my body like in an X-ray machine. I felt hands come inside my body and I could feel somebody massaging my organs. That was Jesus healing my body. The Holy Spirit told me to get up and call someone, and He also told me who to call. So I called my auntie Kandice. Jesus (the Holy Spirit) told me to call Kandice because she was not going to judge me, she was going to care for me and understand why I did what I did as well as take me to the hospital.

I went to the hospital and told the doctors why I took the pills. The doctors could not believe that I had taken the pills three days prior and was still alive; therefore they wanted to draw some blood. When I arrived at the hospital

I remember seeing a homeless man there and he was really cutting up (acting bad). He looked up and saw me and said, "God is right there on your shoulder, you are blessed, you are a beautiful, blessed person. God is right there, he is right there, don't you see Him!" Everyone else in the hospital was looking at the man like he was crazy but me and Kandice after knowing what had just happened both said, "God is with us!" I began thanking God for not giving up on me, even when I wanted to give up on myself.

As I look back over my life, I now see that God was always there for me. The devil was constantly trying to take me out (of course with my help) and God has always been there to see me through. God gave be a brief recap of my whole life up to this point and literally showed me how in spite of my wrong choices in life, He was always there to see me through. I just didn't recognize it back then. My testimony is once I realized and believed that God was real, and that He has been working for me since I was born. I began to see Him and recognize Him for who He is, "my Lord and Savior." God is truly amazing! I used to hear Him but now I listen!

Maurice Horne

I was healed at the age of 29 of a Lymphoma, which is a type of cancer. It was called a "Diffuse Mixed Cell Non Hodgkin's Lymphoma". I was diagnosed at Metropolitan Hospital in Detroit. I had a feeling of disbelief. At the time I was diagnosed I was serving as the Pastor of a church and I didn't smoke or drink. It was like a nightmare to me. I didn't really react to it. I had a horrible feeling as I watched my family react to the news, especially my mother. My mother was so heartbroken over my having cancer, she cried every time she saw me.

The doctor recommended that I begin chemotherapy immediately. I followed his advice and began chemotherapy immediately. I prayed like never before. I was in danger of dying so I knew that I needed God to answer my prayers. I prayedforhealingwithoutmehavingtotakechemotherapy, but if I had to take it then I was willing.

God answered my prayers, but it wasn't as simple as that. On my first chemotherapy treatment I had a bad reaction to the chemotherapy. I was sick for five days. I felt nauseous, I was vomiting, and I had diarrhea. It felt like I was dying. It was such a bad experience that I refused to take another treatment. I felt that if I had to be sick for five days and be well for two days and then begin the cycle all over again, then that would not be a good quality of life for me. The doctor advised me that if I didn't continue to take the treatments that I would die within six months to a year.

I began fasting and praying for my healing. My lymph glands were swollen under my neck, and under my arms. As time passed, they got bigger and bigger. After about 9 months of no chemotherapy my lymph glands were very big and I was in a lot of pain as a result of my lymph glands swelling and blocking my kidney, which made my kidneys swell. I got so sick that I could barely walk because I was not able to grunt or push out my bowels. I was also unable to lie down because it increased my pain which forced me to sit in a chair with a pillow on my stomach while trying to sleep. The pain was so excruciating that I was unable to sleep for long periods of time. I might have gotten an hour of sleep at a time at the most. I had to take laxatives to help my bowels move, which at times took three or four days.

After a while I began contemplating suicide. When others became aware of my cancer I was treated as if I had a contagious disease. I went 11 months without chemotherapy and I could feel myself dying. It was getting very critical because the doctors told me if my kidneys shut down I would not be able to take the chemotherapy because I needed my kidneys to function so I could urinate and eliminate the chemotherapy. After much prayer and consultation with my doctor I decided to begin chemotherapy again. Within two weeks of taking chemotherapy, all of my swollen lymph glands had almost disappeared. I continued taking chemotherapy for one year. It was the most difficult journey I had ever experienced. After taking chemotherapy for one full year, I finished in December of 1985.

By March of 1986, I was diagnosed with another type of cancer. This one was called a Modular Non-Hodgkin's Lymphoma. The doctors wanted to give me a bone marrow transplant. That procedure would have caused me to have to live in a bubble, quarantined from my family, loved ones, and friends because my immune system would no longer function. After much research, I decided against a bone marrow transplant and I received radiation treatments for the next three months. I received the radiation treatments in 1987 and the cancer has been in remission ever since.

Even though I endured much hardship during my bout with cancer, my prayers were answered. My healing means a lot to me because I was only 29 when I first got sick. The doctors told me I probably would not live to see my 30th birthday. In March of 2024 I turned 69 years old. I have lived 40 years beyond what the doctors expected me to live. I am very grateful to God's mercy and grace. I would love to live a long life and reach a ripe age of 80 or 85 years old. But if I never wake up to see another day, I have no complaints because God has been good to me. I now always count my blessings instead of my miseries.

My experience with cancer has changed my life dramatically. First of all I no longer take life for granted, I hold no grudges against anyone, and I never procrastinate about anything. I realize how short life can be. Most of all I take time out to always smell the flowers. Sometimes we can be so busy in life with the many demands upon us that we don't take time to smell the flowers. Smelling the flowers and enjoying time with my family and friends are high priorities with me.

I would have never survived my journey with cancer without God, and without all the prayers that went up on my behalf. I have had the opportunity to share my story with many people that were in the middle of battling cancer. I was able to encourage and inspire them to hold on to God's unchanging hand. I believe God heals through modern medicine as well as without modern medicine. Many people say they wish they could have lived in the days of Jesus to see how Jesus healed miraculously without medicine. But I believe the people in Jesus' day would have loved to have been able to see how God has blessed the world with modern medicine and technology as we have today. God is a healer, and God chooses when and whom He will heal. I am so glad that God chose to heal me!

About the author

Dr. Darryl K. Horne gave his life to Christ at a very early age. He was brought up in the church. His main teacher is the Holy Spirit and only puts to paper what the Holy spirit instructs him too.

He is the founder ovf Harrison's Construction and Home Improvements, Divine Prevention Ministries, and Divine Prevention Ministries Trade School.

He received a BS degree from Michigan State University in 1986, a MSM and MBA degree from Walsh College in 2000 and 2001 and in 2017 earned his PhD from the University of Phoenix.

He is married to his college sweetheart. They are blessed to have three children and 2 grandchildren.

Dr. Horne grew up on the Eastside of Detroit. He is the youngest of 11 children—five sisters and five brothers. He is most excited about being a disciple of Christ and looks forward to sharing with others what the Holy Spirit prompts him to share either in person, or some other spiritually led form of media. His personal life experiences has proven to him without a shadow of a doubt, God is real and resides in all of us. By sharing his testimony, he can help other renew their mind in Christ. God is waiting to hear from you!

Please visit www.divinepreventionministries.org

If you would like Dr. Darryl K. Horne to visit your church and personally share his. Also please consider becoming a sponsor by making an online donation. All donations and moneys are greatly appreciated and used 100% to fund the ministry.

For more information: Email: info@divinepreventionministries.org or visit online at www.divinepreventionministries.org